£2

Racing
Skipper

Mike Golding

Racing
Skipper

Mike Golding

fernhurst
B O O K S

First published 1999 by Fernhurst Books
Duke's Path, High Street, Arundel, West Sussex, BN18 9AJ, UK
Tel: 01903 882277, Fax: 01903 882715,
Email: sales@fernhurstbooks.co.uk.
Contact the publisher for a free, full-colour brochure
or surf the website: www.fernhurstbooks.co.uk

Printed and bound in Hong Kong

British Library Cataloguing in Publication Data:
A catalogue record for this book is available from the British
Library
ISBN 1 898660 57 3

Cover design by Simon Balley
Cover photographs courtesy of Group 4
Design and DTP by Creative Byte of Poole
Printed via World Print

Acknowledgements
The publisher and author gratefully acknowledge the help of Group 4,
and the Centre *for* High Performance Development Ltd., Hartley
Wintney, Hants. Farr International kindly provided the polars of the
Mumm 36, and the photos of the TRI-BUCKLE were provided by
Morglasco Ltd, Bosbora, Mount George Road, Penelewey, Feock,
Truro, TR3 6QX, Tel: 01872 870139.

The book also uses some material from Racing Skipper by Robin
Aisher. The photos of the Mumm 36 were taken by Chris Davies and
the crew was Mike Golding, Simon Walker, Pete Jones, Jo Wright,
Boris Webber, Miles Amin, Mark Hopking and Paul Bennett. The
boat was kindly loaned by Peter Morton of Farr International.
Alison Smith kindly manned the RIB. The photo of the Group 4 team
is courtesy of Roy Stemman, Citigate Publishing, and Team Group 4's
navigation station is coutesy of Mark Pepper/MPP.

Contents

See also the companion volume
Racing Crew by Malcolm McKeag,
also published by Fernhurst.

Introduction

I have been around the world with the author of this book three times. Not literally, I hasten to add, but as his sponsor. Throughout that time, Mike Golding has impressed me as an individual of remarkable courage, tremendous fortitude and great determination. I have seldom met an individual with such strength of character and vision.

But these attributes, I venture to suggest, are of little use unless they are also coupled with experience and technique. Mike Golding has those, too, in good measure, having acquired them the hard way – by learning from experience.

There is something else that is remarkable about Mike Golding. He has the ability to lead others to success and to achieve it himself single-handedly.

I first met him when my Group decided to become a sponsor of ocean racing and began our campaign by signing up for Sir Chay Blyth's British Steel Challenge, an east-west circumnavigation. Like other sponsors, we had no control over the choice of Skipper or 13 crew members who would sail our yacht, and it was Mike Golding, a former fireman, who was assigned to us.

Time proved that to be a fortuitous turn of events, and it was the start of a powerful partnership. Mike and his crew sailed *Group 4* magnificently round the world, coming home in second place just 90 minutes behind the overall leader, despite having been out of the race for 48 hours for repairs.

Four years later, using the same 67-foot all-steel Group 4 yacht, a new crew repeated the exercise. This time, in an extended race – the BT Global Challenge, they won five of the six legs and sailed into Southampton some two days ahead of their nearest rival.

Between these two races, Mike persuaded me to allow him to modify *Group 4* and sail her single-handedly, non-stop, east-west around the world in an attempt on the unbeaten record which Sir Chay Blyth had established over 21 years earlier. For me, sailing is about excitement and meeting a challenge, of overcoming obstacles and demonstrating the astonishing power of the human spirit to cope with extremes of weather and intolerable conditions. It is also about teamwork. But, as chairman of a Group whose business philosophy and focus are based on safety and security, I needed to be sure that Mike Golding could fulfill his ambition with the minimum of danger.Once Mike had explained the modifications he planned to make and the measures he would introduce to complete the voyage safely and successfully, I had no hesitation in giving him the go-ahead. Not only did he sail into the record books but he even knocked over 100 days off Sir Chay Blyth's record.

Three successful circumnavigations would be enough for most people but not for Mike Golding. In 1998 we sponsored the build of a state of the art Open 60 yacht – *Team Group 4* – in which Mike planned to compete in two single-handed round the world races – the Around Alone 1998/99 and the VendJe Globe 2000/01. After a record-breaking first leg of the Around Alone event in which Mike set two world records – the fastest leg ever and the first Briton to win a leg of the race since its inception – he set off on leg two as overall race leader. Sadly, damage to the yacht off the New Zealand coast at the end of leg two put him out of the race but the experience he gained will be extremely useful in later ventures.

Experience is something Mike Golding is keen to share with others, as he does in the pages of this book. I can think of no better companion to guide you to success.

Jørgen Philip-Sørensen
Chairman
Group 4 Securitas (International) B.V.

1 Crews and teams

The key to becoming a successful yacht racing skipper lies in your ability to manage your boat and your crew. Your approach to management will determine your enjoyment, as well as your crew's, and also your success on the race course.

This book is not designed to teach you to sail, but concentrates on how to skipper well. Skippering is about managing both the boat and the team. It is not critical that the skipper is the best sailor on board. It is critical, however, that the skipper extracts the best from each crew member and utilises ALL the experience that exists.

So often a good collection of sailors fail to succeed solely because they lack the focus that a good racing skipper can engender within his team. It is also important that, while managing, the skipper gains the trust and respect of the crew to ensure they give their best performance come race day.

> The secret of running a good team is to keep the six guys who hate your guts away from the seven who aren't yet sure.

The team that won the BT Global Challenge – 22 people to co-ordinate.

The biggest single performance boost a racing yacht can get is from its crew.

The following pages set out techniques which have helped me to run both happy and successful yacht crews in campaigns ranging from round the cans to round the world yacht races. These techniques remain the same however long the course and however large or small the yacht.

FINDING THE BEST CREW

The commitment and attitude of the team members will make or break the success of any yacht racing campaign. If you have a core of people who sail with you regularly, you will already have a stable base on which to build. Try to add others with experience of the type of boat you are racing.

If you are starting from scratch, then choosing crew will be the most important factor in ensuring a successful and enjoyable project.

Whatever, I would always look for people who fit the following criteria:

- Can sail
- Have enthusiasm
- Show commitment
- Have ability to "grunt up"
- Are sociable

To get a good team together requires the right mix of people, and in selecting your crew it would be a mistake to look only for those with sailing talent. A far better solution is to pick the sort of people you want to sail with, possibly adding talented sailors who are both willing and able to pass on their skills to those around them. It is vital that no matter how deep your desire to win, you don't allow the boat to be run by prima donnas who will spoil the fun and ruin your chances of real success. Sailing should be FUN.

On the British Steel and BT Global Challenge round the world yacht races, the skippers did not have the luxury of selecting our crews. Each skipper was allocated crew members who had paid to take part in the race. Many had little or no sailing experience but they were collectively trained to a basic standard by The Challenge Business

before going on to what were called 'placement sails'. During these sails, the crew members were divided into the three key areas of the boat - bow, mast and cockpit, to assess their aptitude for each position.

A good crewman can always find something to improve or to fix.

Skippers and crews met for the first time at the London Boat Show nine months before the start of the race and from that moment onwards it was the responsibility of the individual skipper to extract the best from the allocated team. The levels of enthusiasm and commitment shown by these crew members was remarkable, given the fact that many were spending time away from their families and taking breaks from their careers.

Enthusiasm and commitment are the most effective tools on which to build a new team - the rest is just time and training.

SPECIALIST OR JACK-OF-ALL-TRADES?

In general I prefer to have crew members who are keen to specialise, rather than those who would prefer to do everything. This gives the individual real ownership of a task, empowering them and giving them responsibility for the outcome.

It's helpful to divide the crew positions into the three **areas** of the boat - bow, mast and cockpit. The dream team would consist of a crew that naturally divided into these three areas.

Bow

This is a job for the bold and brave. The Bow often has to work alone and yet be part of the foredeck team. From the bow it is often difficult to see or hear what is going on in the cockpit - never mind understand the logic of some of the decisions! A good foredeck crew need some attitude but not too much! Many young sailors get their breaks on the bow and see it as a stepping stone towards the back of the boat. Foredeck crew should be quick-witted, light, strong and, most important of all, nimble on their feet.

Mast

A good mast person is someone who can either go forward to help the Bow or come aft to assist in the cockpit. Physical strength and knowledge of sail trim are definite advantages because the job includes sweating up and taking down sails as well as adjusting all the sail and pole controls at the mast. Weight is less of a factor in the middle of the boat, but the ability to be nimble on their feet is still a significant advantage.

Cockpit

In the cockpit you will need Trimmers, Grinders, Mainsheet, Pit, Helm and a Navigator/Tactician/Strategist. Depending on the size of boat, these form the afterguard and to some extent the 'brains trust' of the boat.

The idea is that the Trimmers, Grinders and Mainsheet make sure that the sail plan is giving maximum power all the time, while the Helm puts the power to best effect on the race course. These people need to be working together very closely and must trust each other's judgement.

The Pit can be viewed as the centre of operations. Located in the main hatchway of most boats the Pit is surrounded by all the halyard tails, pole controls and trimming controls. A good Pit is also the key to good communications from the front to the back of the boat.

The Helm is locked into speed, concentrating on the instruments (at the mast) and the genoa telltales.

The Helm should primarily be concerned with speed to the next mark.

A Tactician is needed to tell the Helm where to go and to discuss the various tactical and navigational options. In many cases the Tactician will also be the mainsheet trimmer, but in any case it is essential that there is good synergy between these three key positions on the boat. It is also useful for the Tactician and Mainsheet to be competent helms, giving more options for rotation during longer races.

Helm and Bow may appear to be glamorous jobs, and often you get several takers for these and none for the middle of the boat. It should be made clear however that the Helm needs the ability to endure long periods of intense concentration and remain completely focused and not be distracted by general conversations among the rest of the crew. Similarly the Bow not only climbs to the end of the pole and spikes the spinnaker - they also have to sit at the front of the line-up on the rail with the least protection. On long races this can be very arduous.

The Tactician is in constant conversation with the Helm. They watch the course, the chart and the compass. This Tactician has a hand-held Deckman computer.

The Bow.

The Mast.

The Pit.

*The mainsheet person controls the mainsheet,
mainsheet fine tune, traveller, checkstay,
the runner and the topmast backstay. He is
in constant communication with the helm.*

Eyes in the boat

What your crew focus their attention on during a race is of vital importance. In general, crew members will have their eyes (or their concentration) either in or out of the boat. 'Eyes in' means concentrating on sail trim and the general status of crew activity. 'Eyes out' means watching for other boats, tactical options, windshifts, increases and decreases in wind pressure and awkward waves. Generally the idea is to give the Helm additional sets of eyes.

A good Bow has their eyes out of the boat and needs to read the course ahead, watching any boats ahead go round marks and deducing what's going to be needed well ahead of time. The Bow should read the sailing instructions (as should every crew member) so they know what is going on round the course - remember, once racing, good communications between the back and the front can be very difficult at times, even on small boats.

Similarly, the Helm and Navigator need their eyes out of the boat. Crew in the middle of the boat should have their eyes in the boat. The Mainsheet, in assisting the Helm, needs to have eyes everywhere!

This is by no means a definitive list of crew positions but rather a guide as to how to start thinking about people power, no matter how large the crew or yacht. What you must achieve is a job specification for each and every crew member. Everyone should be contributing something and everyone should have ownership of their job, both on the water when racing and during the pre-race preparation. Every job on the boat contributes to the yacht's success and a good skipper will ensure that the crew know they recognise the importance of every crew position. If you want to win, carry no passengers.

CHOOSING YOUR TEAM

With this outline specification you will now have a better chance of selecting a balanced crew from those who want to sail with you.

Get details of each person's sailing experience and find out if they've got the skills you're looking for. Don't worry too much, provided the person can sail. It's really all about

attitude. Attitude, as Sir Chay Blyth defined it for the
BT Global Challenge crews, encompasses three factors :

Attitude
- Anticipate - are you ready for the next move?
- Detail   - pay attention to the small things
- Speed   - if you do it, do it quickly

Each has to be practised, practised, practised.

From attitude comes .....

Style
- Be aware
- Look the part, feel the part

Which leads to .....

Professionalism
- Do it fast
- Do it now
- Do it right

These factors are what you're looking for as you go into the
crew interview stage.

As with any other interview, first impressions will tell you
half the story. Was the individual punctual and presentable?
Can you see yourself spending your leisure time with this
person? The way they answer your questions will speak
volumes about their enthusiasm and commitment. Also, do
they want to do the job you're offering? What do they
expect to gain from joining your campaign? Do they have
the same agenda as you - do you want an all-out-to-win
season or a more balanced year?

Even if fun is your main criteria, you are going racing
and things will go wrong, so the ability to 'grunt up' is
important. Someone's got to volunteer to go up the mast
to retrieve a halyard in Force 6.

Structure your interview in such a way that you can make
good comparisons between individuals. Work out the
balance that is needed to achieve your goals and then
take the shortlist sailing - with no commitment either way.
Don't forget you're being assessed too!

TRIAL SAIL

This is probably best done as a training sail rather than
a race. A short windward-leeward course is best.

Your goals are to :

- Treat the session as you would a race
- Practise manoeuvres - tacks, gybes, mark roundings
- Identify problems
- See if the candidates can cope with the gear on the boat

Make regular stops for discussion, seeking ideas for
improvement. Encourage your prospective crew members
to contribute, especially in their own area of speciality.
The contributions made at this stage will give you an
excellent idea of their ability and suitability.

The initial windward / leeward course might be half a mile
(depending on the size of boat). Gradually shorten this as
you get better and apply more pressure. Seek to improve
continuously. At the end of this short, focused session you
should have a much better idea who you want on board,
and they'll know if they want to sail with you!

2 Leadership

Assemble the people, then build and run the team.

There is no difference between leading an amateur crew and a professional one. Both groups are individuals with different needs and abilities. If you create the right agenda then a common purpose will give the crew a natural discipline. Crew members who are forced to change from their normal roles or techniques should be encouraged to realise that it is not about personalities but about the pursuit of continuous improvement.

So what is leadership in this context? I've given this a lot of thought, and even lectured on the subject! I believe that once you've assembled your team, the essential elements of leadership are building and running the team.

BUILDING THE TEAM

- Get to know each other
- Set a shared goal
- Allocate jobs clearly
- Gather and share information
- Be bold and decisive
- Be a pioneer

How do you build your team?

The development of a team involves a mixture of training and socialising - both are equally important. **Make sure, however, that it is clear which is which.** Training is **not** socialising and when you're sail training it should be no different from the way you'd sail during a race.

Socialising allows everyone to get to know each other better, which invariably makes a difference on the water. A group of people who know each other well will always perform better than those who don't.

Early on, set a clear goal for the project. This may well be 'to be the best we can be'. Everything then follows from this. Even a low key campaign needs a goal - such as 'to be better than we are now' - that gives everyone something to work towards. If the crew have differing individual agendas you'll have to sort that out or agree to part company. You can't go forward without a shared common goal.

As skipper, always look at yourself first. If your goal is to have the best team, you may have to move yourself from your favoured position on the yacht if there's someone on board who can do the job better. It is rewarding watching your crew achieve good results as a direct result of your organisation and planning.

For example, in the 1995 Admiral's Cup I was skipper of the Mumm 36 *Group 4* and yet didn't steer during inshore events as I was not the best helm on board for this type of event. The same can be said for some of Peter Blake's and Dennis Conner's campaigns. However, if you elect for a lower-key approach and are determined to steer, then build a suitable team around you and make it clear to your crew that your agenda is to become a better, more experienced helm.

RUNNING THE TEAM

- Give clear briefings
- Continually review performance
- Avoid the blame culture
- Show empathy (put yourself into the shoes of your crew • and respond to individual needs)
- Avoid the rumour culture (say it to their face, not behind their back)

How do you run your team ?

During the BT Global Challenge skipper training we were introduced to the John Adair leadership model. This emphasises the need for a leader to juggle their time between the task, the team and the individual's needs.

Within the John Adair model (page 21), you need to be able to move seamlessly between the three circles. Try not to spend too much time on tasks (you have a crew to do that) but concentrate on organising the team and encouraging each individual. Try to leave time for eating, sleeping and breathing!

Briefing the crew.
Before you set off make sure
everyone knows the agenda.

On my boat I prefer to be informed of each and every sail change, every manoeuvre, every significant change in the weather and every major problem. This is so I can keep a handle on the overall plan: imagine coming on deck to find that while you were asleep the boat tacked four times and shortened sail by 50%. You'd definitely have lost the plot!

The way we would handle sail changes during the BT Global Challenge is that I'd be called, we'd monitor the conditions for a short time and then decide whether to go for a change or not. However, on a boat of this size with a crew of 14, the skipper doesn't have to be on deck for the actual change.

Lengthy delays in decision making lead to anxiety or even fear among the crew, so work closely with your watch leaders and teach them when you want to be called.

In short, I want to control the things I know more about than my crew. Ultimately, the skipper is responsible whatever the situation.

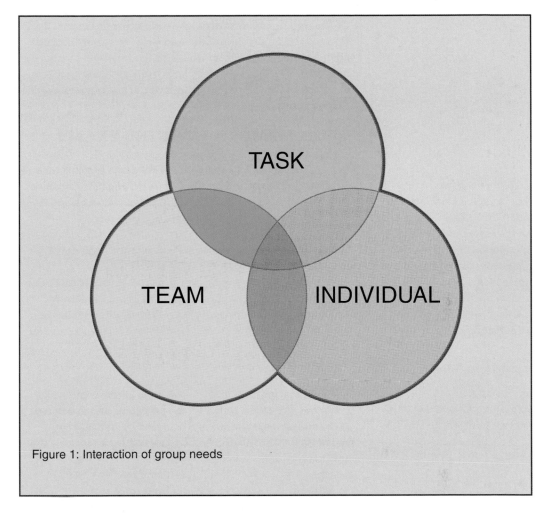

Figure 1: Interaction of group needs

What do you do when things go wrong?

I'm a great believer in the 'no blame culture'. When things
go wrong look ahead to overcome the problem, rather than
targeting someone for blame. Fix the foul-up, learn from the
experience and then leave it on the wave behind.

Yacht racing is about achieving objectives. When things do
go wrong, blame should not be targeted at any individual.
Achieving the objective is a team effort and as such the
whole team should take responsibility for any incident and
learn from the experience. Engendering a sense of humour
at such times always helps by deflecting attention away
from the individual and towards the task at hand and the
team's need to prevail.

*Centre for High
Performance Development
Ltd (CHPD) specialises
in the assessment and
development of
behaviour to enhance
the effectiveness of
individuals and teams
and improve the success
of organisations.

On one top boat there was an horrific error on the foredeck. When it was finally sorted out and everyone was lined up again on the rail the Helm whacked the Mainsheet Trimmer next to him. "What's that for?" he grunted. "Pass it on!" came the reply - a poignant reminder of the whole crew's responsibility.

WHAT MAKES A WINNING TEAM?

In management terms, winners exhibit High Performance Behaviours. Described by the *Centre for High Performance Development**, these are behaviours that will enhance an individual, team or organisation's performance.

Set out below are eleven High Performance Behaviours researched and endorsed by the *Centre for High Performance Development* over the last two decades. These were further validated during the BT Global Challenge when the race was used as a case study for leadership and team building factors crucial for survival and performance at the highest level and in extremely difficult and changeable conditions.

The findings, which outline the lessons learned and what made the difference between the 14 yachts and their crew, make fascinating reading and above all prove that the use of High Performance Behaviours really can make a winning team.

As skipper, you should try to get your team to adopt behaviours that produce outstanding performance.

HIGH PERFORMANCE BEHAVIOURS

Information Search - Gathers many different kinds of information and uses a wide variety of sources to build a rich informational environment in preparation for decision-making. Particularly: yacht performance, sea conditions and weather data.

Concept Formation - Builds frameworks or models, forms concepts, hypotheses or ideas on the basis of information. Becomes aware of patterns, trends and cause/effect relations by linking disparate information.

Conceptual Flexibility - Identifies feasible alternatives or multiple options in planning and decision-making. Holds different options in focus simultaneously and evaluates their pros and cons. Explores all the options before taking a decision.

Empathy - Uses open and probing questions, summaries and paraphrasing to understand the ideas, concepts and feelings of another. Can comprehend events, issues, problems and opportunities from the viewpoint of others.

Teamwork - Involves others and is able to build co-operative teams in which group members feel valued and empowered and have shared goals. Avoids the blame culture.

Developing People - Creates a positive climate in which people increase the accuracy of their own strengths and limitations. Provides coaching, training and developmental resources to improve performance.

Influence - Uses a variety of methods (eg persuasive arguments, modelling behaviour, inventing symbols, forming alliances and appealing to the interest of others) to gain support for ideas and strategies and values.

Building Confidence - States own 'stand' or position on issues; unhesitatingly takes decisions when required and commits self and others accordingly. Expresses confidence in the future success of the actions to be taken. Recognises and rewards people for their contributions.

Presentations - Presents ideas clearly, with ease and interest so that the other person (or audience) understands what is being communicated. Uses technical, symbolic, non-verbal and visual aids effectively.

Pro-activity - Structures the task for the team. Implements plans and ideas. Takes responsibility for all aspects of the situation even beyond ordinary boundaries - and for the success and failure of the group.

Continuous Improvement - Possesses high internal work standards and sets ambitious, risky and yet attainable goals. Wants to do things better, to improve, to be more effective and efficient. Measures progress against targets.

3 Training and motivation

We touched on training in the first chapter. Now let's look in more detail at how you are going to develop your crew and keep them motivated.

A good training schedule fits the ability of the crew. There is no point in doing something too difficult that might damage the boat or even worse a crew member. Training is mainly about manoeuvres - it's manoeuvres that catch you out on the race course. Boatspeed can come later. In fact you can't easily work on boatspeed unless you have another boat to sail against.

Start with a training sail. You'll soon get a feel for what people can do. Then devise your programme with a logical progression, but keeping an element of fun.

Your sailing sessions should be :

- Short - not more than half a day. (If you have longer you need a target, eg to sail somewhere.)
- Clearly defined
- Well structured
- Organised around an agenda and an objective - it's vital everyone knows why you're training
- Sailed as though you're racing

Remember to include a debrief at the end of each manoeuvre or exercise.

On the dock, develop games that help familiarise the crew with the yacht and its operation, as well as developing the crew's agility and physique with activities such as :

- Identifying every skin fitting or item of safety equipment on board

- Timed competitions to get the spinnaker on deck and raised to the top of the mast in its bag

The ideas are limitless, but make whatever you do fun - people will learn more.

TRAINING

- There should be no difference between practice and racing. Make practice sessions as realistic as possible. After all, racing offshore you will need the crew to raise their game despite the absence of other visible yachts

- Work at each manoeuvre, starting with the simple and progressing to the more complex. With each exercise find the best way for your team, then stick to it developing techniques to improve speed and efficiency. If you do it differently every time the team will never have the chance to perfect the manoeuvre

- Even if you seem to have good boatspeed, you must encourage the view that the best crew win because they make fewest mistakes

- Set realistic and attainable targets

- During training sessions, it will help if you stand back and watch the crew without getting too deeply engrossed in the activity. You'll see more

- Be seen to be leading from the front. Spend some time working in each crew position on the boat. Only by doing this will you truly appreciate the complexity and difficulty of each crew member's role

- Swapping crew positions gives everyone an appreciation of the other guy's point of view

- Learn from your mistakes. During training, if things go wrong then take the opportunity to help everyone learn from the experience. For example, suppose you get a twist in the spinnaker; work through the reasons and the best way to do it in the future

Encourage everyone to talk about their own job - even if someone made a mistake. Enthusiasm and a willingness to learn are the critical attributes for future success.

After a sailing session get the crew to watch a training video to promote discussion, or have crew members prepare presentations, eg how to tack the boat, or how weather systems work. This gets away from the skipper always being the teacher, with everything revolving around him. It's better if people take responsibility for their own learning.

A lot of basic knowledge can be acquired through selected reading and everyone should be encouraged to learn :

- Theory of sailing
- Nautical jargon
- Safety
- Man overboard procedure
- Abandon ship procedure and basic sea survival
- Rules of the Road and Racing Rules
- Fundamental yacht systems
- Navigation (as in the RYA Yachtmaster syllabus)
- Basic signals
- Basic radio procedures
- Mooring and anchoring
- Sail plan options
- Sail trimming
- Reefing
- Spinnaker handling

On my yachts I like to produce a manual that has, for each manoeuvre, an agreed role and list of tasks for each person. For a big crew this is duplicated because you will have more than one watch. This manual also has all the details for the race, (race instructions, weather charts etc) as well our pre-race weather and tidal strategy.

There should also be a section on polar performance. Polar diagrams give the Helm and Trimmers the target boatspeed, true wind angle and VMG (velocity made good). They are often the only way of gauging performance when offshore and are an excellent starting point for a crew in training. By comparing performance against that predicted in the polar it is possible to measure improvements and assess the performance of different Helms and Trimmers.

Polar diagrams are a method of finding out the target speed you should be aiming for in any given true wind speed and true wind angle. Fairly good polars can normally be obtained from the designer of the boat or extrapolated from the IMS certificate of IMS-rated yachts. Polars are tables of performance which have normally been calculated, rather than taken from empirical measurement. As such, they will need to be modified so they best represent your boat's actual performance on the water.

Polar information is great provided you have spent the time calibrating your boat's instruments - boatspeed, true wind speed and true wind angle need to be accurate for the predictions to be of any value. Keep a record on board of all the base calibration settings for your instrument system - if the power goes down one night you may be able to recover your instrument calibration if you have this information to hand.

A polar diagram (page 28) consists of a semicircular graph in which the concentric semicircles indicate boatspeed and the true wind angles from head-to-wind at zero degrees (straight up) to dead downwind at 180 degrees (straight down).

Each curve represents the predicted polar speed possible for a given true wind speed and true wind angle. Each curve is in fact two curves, one upwind with fore and aft sails and one downwind with a spinnaker. The crossover between the two curves shows the true wind angle where the sail change from one to the other should occur.

The small squares show optimum upwind and downwind performance. This is the boatspeed and true wind angle at which the boat should theoretically attain maximum upwind or downwind VMG.

The VMG can be taken off the polar by taking a line from the peak of the curve across to the speed scale at 90 degrees. The boatspeed is taken by following the concentric circles around to the speed scale.

Other tables can be used to help find optimum upwind and downwind information quickly. These simply break down the polars into more easily used tables which can also include information such as the optimum heel angle, optimum tacking or gybing angles and leeway as well as predicted apparent wind angle. Much can be learned and

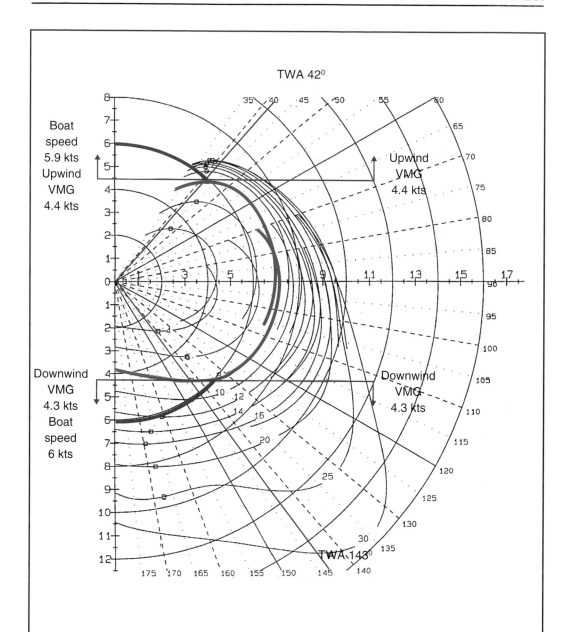

A typical polar diagram - in this case a Mumm 36.
For wind speeds between 4 and 30 knots.
The square datam points shown at each curve indicate optimum upwind and downwind
speed and angles

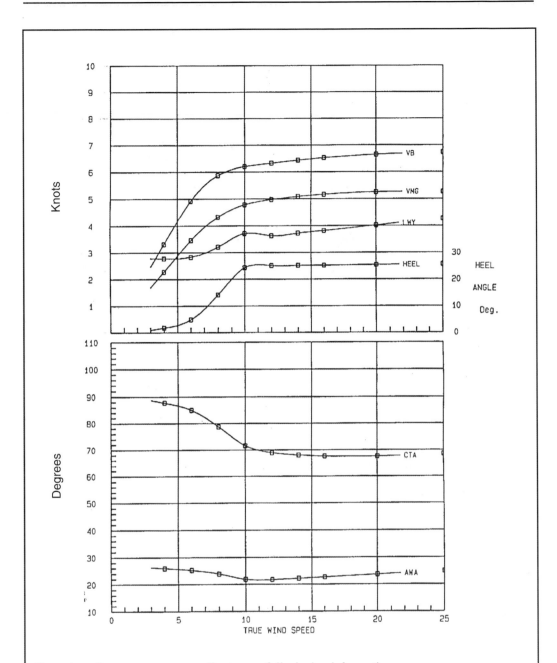

*These two diagrams are an excellent way of displaying information
on optimum upwind performance.*

*VB = Velocity of Boat. VMG = Velocity Made Good. LWY = Leeway. Heel = Optimum Heel Angle.
CTA = Calculated Tacking Angle. AWA = Apparant Wind Angle.*

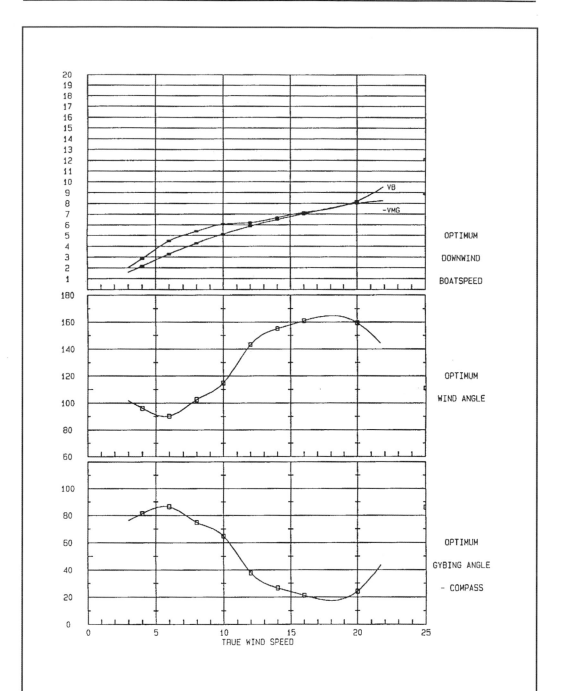

These three diagrams are an excellent way of displaying information
on optimum downwind performance.

VB = Velocity of Boat. VMG = Velocity Made Good.

gained by understanding these methods of mapping your boat's performance.

You should spend a lot of time refining your boat's polar and performance tables. It is an ongoing process which is never finished but time spent evaluating performance and your team's improvement is time well spent.

When you get out on the water and start racing remember that performance polars are giving you a theoretical target. If on race day a similar boat consistently seems to gain on you upwind, determine whether or not they are sailing their boat higher and slower or lower and faster. Check and compare your sail trim with that of the gaining boat and if this doesn't help adjust your own height to suit and see if this stops the rot.

If this consistently seems to work you can modify your polars accordingly, but beware of modifying them too quickly and making them unattainable in normal conditions. Polars should provide you with a ready reference for your best upwind, downwind and reaching speeds - they should also be realistic and repeatable targets for you and your crew to aspire to.

In addition to the polar performance data, build up a good sail change diagram listing the point at which each sail change should occur. This should be based on the maximum and minimum wind strengths in which each sail can be flown and what maintains the best speed in practice. Again it takes a long time in a range of conditions to get this right but the work will pay off when trying to make the difficult decision about changing up or down during a race. It seldom pays to take a sail outside its range. As well as the risk of potential damage to the sail it is often not fast and can cause gear failure. Judging the minimum wind speed at which a sail remains fast is just as vital as judging the point at which to change down. So take care to focus on the lower as well as the upper limit.

SPECIFIC TRAINING TOPICS

Yacht racing is a huge subject and there are thousands of topics to choose from to provide interesting and varied training. But before you can begin to tackle the more complex subjects you need your crew to have the basics.

Just arriving and leaving the dock might be a good starting point! There's nothing worse than doing this in a sloppy way, and it sets the tone for the rest of the day.

You'll also need to improve you crew's knowledge of :

- Hoisting, lowering and packing sails
- Sail care
- Rope care
- Sailing upwind
- Tacking
- Reaching
- Spinnaker preparation and.....
- Hoisting
- Trimming
- Gybing
- Dropping - float drops, windward drops and foredeck drops
- Manoeuvres under sail

Whatever you do you must expect things to go wrong during training - that's what it's for! On one training session on *Group 4* we were practising a spinnaker peel when we noticed a large ship about two miles away. Plenty of time, but it was definitely on a collision course. We were all trying new crew positions for the first time so I started to apply the pressure for a fast peel and gybe to get clear. With a fair breeze the distance between *Group 4* and the ship was closing rapidly.

This was turning into an exercise too far. We needed to work very fast. We always had the option of taking the spinnaker down but although I certainly would never advocate the risk, I believed our crew was good enough to deliver under pressure. The crew who could see the obvious need for urgency rose to the challenge, peeling and gybing **just** in time as we passed under the ship's stern. Looking up, I noticed the ship's pilot was a friend of mine, and was surprised that he'd kept up his speed and a dead straight course.

By coincidence he was in our local that night, and I tackled him on his callousness.

'No problem' he replied. 'I told them: "That's Mike Golding. He knows what he's doing. We'll just keep going".'

If only he knew!

USING PROFESSIONALS

One way to speed up the learning process is to bring in the services of an experienced professional racing sailor to help with your crew training. You need an individual (or individuals) who can show you how to prepare, train on and race your boat.

Paul Stanbridge *(Toshiba)* and Steve Hayles *(Silk Cut)* fulfilled this role admirably on *Group 4*. The crew not only learned technique, but also saw their professional approach. Some might feel that this would undermine the skipper's position but I contest that it shows a high degree of self confidence and commitment to the team goal.

A professional may also be the link to finding other able and committed sailors who want to join your programme. The cost is relatively small in relation to the cost of the average racing yacht, and compared to how quickly the right person could put you on the right track.

BOATSPEED AND TWO-BOAT TUNING

It's impossible to check your speed without another boat alongside. So try to team up with a similar boat, and participate honestly! The objective is for you both to gain, but even if they don't co-operate fully, it's worth knowing if you're fast or slow.

Upwind it can take ages to get into position. The best way is for the two boats to cross on opposites tacks, with the port tacker ducking the starboard boat's transom and then tacking on her quarter. Now both boats are lined up in clear air and similar tide and you can see who is quickest. In fact you can race to windward, tacking and obeying the normal racing rules. Downwind two-boating is just the same: sail

across the other boat's transom, then gybe onto a parallel
course. Try various alterations to your set up and see which
comes out best.

Use the sessions to compare :

- Speed in a straight line
- Speed through tacks and gybes
- Acceleration out of manoeuvres

Also to :

- Evaluate instrument calibration
- Test and evaluate sail combinations
- Alter rig set up and try different rake and
  prebend positions
- Move the crew weight fore and aft. IMS and many
  modern designs often benefit from having weight
  forward to dig the bows in - maximising waterline
  length and gaining lift from the convex bow shape
  on these types of yachts
- Generate more accurate polars. Begin by using
  the polar information from the yacht's designer
  and modify to improve its reliability

It's a good idea to have an independent person in a RIB who
can assess the differences that can be seen better away
from the boat, eg mainsail and headsail twist.

4 Selecting the boat and the racing area

It will always pay to get the best boat you can while staying within your means. Don't forget that all boats have hidden running costs and make sure that you take this into account. A 'Grand Prix' yacht may budget for as much as twice the cost of the boat, but a conventional handicap yacht may get through the season for a fraction of this.

Perhaps the most important consideration is location: you ideally want to sail close to home, but you may be prepared to travel to find the type of racing you like. Some classes are very specific to certain regions and there's not much point in purchasing a class of yacht where there is no local competition.

A small one design or handicap yacht may provide the opportunity of 'trailer sailing' the boat to regattas nationally or internationally. This would put you on the fast track to gaining competitive experience. Racing in different venues and against different competition will certainly broaden your skills and knowledge. A further consideration is whether you can find the crew for your new boat. Eight people are a lot to manage every weekend; a four-man sportsboat is half the problem.

HANDICAP, ONE DESIGN OR OPEN CLASS RACING?

Handicap

This is probably the most popular type of racing. Most people have different yachts and only good handicapping rules allow these boats to race together and show results that bear a relationship to the ability of the crew. There are many different rules that allow dissimilar boats to race together. Arguably the most highly developed is the International Measurement System (IMS) which, in general, is the preferred handicapping system of the top 'Grand Prix' sailors around the world. IMS is a far more sophisticated system than the predominantly UK based system known as Channel Handicap System (CHS). IMS involves a far more complex measurement process that must be carried out by approved measurers while CHS requires the filling out of a simple form.

In the UK, CHS (now known as IRC) has a very large following and is a rule that on average produces sensible outcomes. However, any handicapping systems can suffer when a boat that fits the rule too closely is allowed to win race after race, simply because the boat does well due to certain optimised design parameters.

The latest development in yacht handicapping is the conception by the RORC and UNCL of IR2000, a new system of measuring and rating with associated time allowances. Under this ruling come two ratings that apply to almost all ballasted monohull yachts throughout the world.

The first rating is the IRC, a direct back-to-back successor to the CHS, which was introduced on 1 January 1999. The IRC addresses the issue of boats being built or modified to fit the rule, as the rating will be reviewed and changed year on year as necessary.

The second rating, IRM, will be introduced from 1 January 2000 and will be a fully published and independently measured rule.

One design

In theory, one design racing is cheap and gives close racing. In practice the top teams can spend fairly big money in the fight for the small advantage needed to get to the front. At this level the crews are generally so good that they become almost one design themselves. It's not uncommon to spend considerable sums of money on the hull of a production 36-footer. This might involve fairing the bottom (even new hulls may need fairing), getting the foils to match the designer's templates and/or optimising their shapes, applying a coat of epoxy and burnishing it as well as recessing all the standard skin fittings. Not all one design classes have owners who go to these extremes; what I'm saying is check to see what

level the competition is going to as this could have a big impact on the budget required to be successful.

There is a great deal to be said for the slower one design yachts, because the separation will be less between the front and the back of the fleet encouraging the development of good sailing skills. This reduced separation also serves to encourage newcomers who may be at the back of the fleet but at least will not turn up at the bar to find everyone else has gone home.

The Mumm 36 is the ultimate one design.

Open class

Open Class is really for the specialist. Unless it is your aim to race shorthanded offshore or transocean, this is probably not for you. The rule, as the name implies, is open. Anything goes so long as it fits within the size limitations.

These boats are fast and developmental, so you can use innovation to get ahead. It is not necessarily the most expensive boat that wins. However it is an expensive area as boat values drop dramatically with each new step forward in design. Designs can be very radical such as *Team Group 4* - an Open 60 Finot-Conq design with wing mast and swing keel. Apart from big multihulls these boats are a blast! Perhaps the fastest monos afloat.

The Open Class is not for the faint-hearted – a swing keel, wing mast and water ballast guarantee you're never bored!

BUILDING NEW?

If you are having a new boat built then it is essential that you oversee the construction and fit-out. You need to visit the yard regularly to ensure you know every aspect of the boat and its construction.

While building *Team Group 4* in France we had our own

project manager on site throughout the build. During the
early construction we elected to add a swing keel and
a wing mast to the original specifications and, in addition,
we removed the electrics from the build contract and
utilised electronic specialists known to us. (In my
experience electronics and electrical installations
can be the downfall of many offshore yachts.)

A good project manager ensures that when different
options arise and the yard need a decision it can be
made on the spot, or referred back to you quickly.
Additionally, the contract can be altered accordingly,
removing hassles later.

All modifications to specification must be referred to the
designer, however old the boat. It's mad to increase the
keel weight and put on a bigger rig without knowing that
the structure can handle it, but people do and are surprised
when the keel falls off.

Don't just pay the designer to do the design. We expect
our designers to keep the project up-to-date with the latest
developments and incorporate new ideas as the build
progresses and, once the boat is on the water, to assist in
the further development of the design.

If you are buying a production boat you may not be able to
control all elements of the build but it would be wise to have
a pre-delivery inspection by a qualified yacht surveyor.

5 Setting up the boat and tuning for speed

One sure way to improve performance of your yacht is to spend time preparing it to be as fast as possible from the word go. This means tackling lots of small details that independently may seem insignificant, but collectively make a pronounced difference.

The Mumm 36 *Group 4* was superbly built, but it took weeks of hard work to get the detail right and even longer to bring her up to 'Grand Prix' level for the Admiral's Cup. Sadly, there was little to be gained because every boat in the Admiral's Cup fleet was prepared to this standard - any boat not worked up like this would be miles off the pace.

Starting from the keel up, the following are the essential elements of your preparation for setting up the boat and tuning for speed.

BOTTOM FINISH AND DETAILING

- All outlets should have flush-fitting seacocks. Mark the handles to ensure they are exactly flush when closed.

- If your yacht is fitted with sacrificial anodes that create turbulence, work out how you can modify or remove them. If you are dry sailing it is quite adequate to have an anode which you hang over the side while on the dock. If your boat is in the water most of the time you will have to work out the best compromise for performance verses longevity.

- Check the class rules to see if you are allowed to fair the legs of the sail drive.

> Never take a flier before you get to the start line. Go with what you know to be fast.

*Fair the sail drive leg
if the rules allow.
Check the folding prop
for correct operation.*

- Folding propellers should fold completely and may have a favoured hydrodynamic position. If so, mark the drive shaft so that this position can be found easily during the pre-start when your engine is shut down.

- Fair the keel and rudder to templates supplied by the designer. The designed shape will be the best starting point and even the best built boats seldom achieve this out of the factory. Any asymmetry will definitely slow the boat. It may also be possible to optimise the shape further, provided the class rules allow.

- The entire hull can be faired if you have the time and money. It's not a complicated job, just a lot of hard work.

- Paint the whole bottom with a fairable epoxy or antifouling that is capable of being burnished back to a smooth finish. Grit of 400-600 is ideal to allow the best possible reduction in friction. A smoother finish will not be any more efficient and may even be slower!

- The rudder blade should fit as closely to the hull as is possible, to improve the 'end plate' effect of the blade.

A well set up rudder has as small a gap as possible between it and the hull. The smaller the gap, the larger the end plate effect – for a given rudder angle the turning effect is maximised.

- The rudder-to-skeg gap may be improved with bonded Mylar flaps to enhance water flow.

- Don't forget the area of the keel and hull which are hidden when the yacht is in its cradle!

- A well-prepared hull is much faster - after all, it's free speed!

PARASITIC WEIGHT

I have a reputation for being fanatical about weight. In some ways that's true. Sailing is a power/weight game and particularly so in one designs. You will almost certainly have more potential to go faster if your boat is lighter. Each extra kilo of weight results in a kilo of water having to be moved several feet out of the way each time the boat travels its own length. On a round the world race that means an extra 2000 tons of water have to be moved aside for each extra kilo. Put that to your crew and they may agree to leave their Walkmen and mobile phones behind.

- Take **everything** off the boat and then clean and dry her.

- Put back on only what you need for the race.

- Where practicable get the crew to share personal items rather than duplicating.

- Give each crew member a list of what they're allowed to bring. Ensure everyone has good quality gear.

- Let it be known that you will carry out random checks on kitbags.

On the BT Global Challenge we reduced the weight of each crew member's kitbag to 9kg, not bad for over 35 days at sea. And there weren't too many complaints!

Water and food

The rules may specify a minimum quantity of water to take. A watermaker may save weight in the long run.

Food is the crew's power supply, so plan for generous portions. If the race is going slower than planned, you can then make two meals into three.

For longer runs, freeze-dried food may save a lot of weight. Vacuum pack into crew meal-sized portion packs for ease of preparation. The menu can be pre-planned on a seven day rotation which is adequate variation.

Have some staple snack foods such as cereal or biscuits available all the time, so nobody gets hungry. Hot drinks should be available as often as required.

On leg one of the British Steel Challenge, when our estimated time of arrival into Rio de Janeiro was less than 24 hours, we enjoyed a feast and deliberately finished the food. Within hours we found ourselves becalmed just miles from the finish line. Thirty hours later a hungry crew arrived in Rio a lot wiser - always leave a little in reserve!

Fuel

Carry the minimum fuel but always be aware that you may need fuel to get out of trouble, rescue a man overboard or even another competitor. Your main engine is a part of your safety equipment and this is not an area to push too far. Increase the efficiency of your charging system so you can run the engine less frequently and save fuel.

Additional gear

Leave the mooring lines and fenders on the dock, or have them shipped to your destination. Get rid of tails on ropes, cushions, even the table, provided the rules allow. Carry only the sails you're going to need and make sure they are dry. High-tech sails save weight, especially aloft.

SAILS

Your sails are your engine. Unfortunately you tend to get what you pay for and the fast ones don't usually last as long as the slow ones.

In one-design never take a flier before you get to the startline. Go with what you know to be fast. Choose a sailmaker who has experience and a track record in your class. Computer Aided Design has made sailmaking

The sails are your engine. Instil in the crew that they must take care of them at all times.

more of a science, enabling sailmakers to reproduce fast shapes more easily. However, even new sails may need recutting to get the best from them and don't assume any one sailmaker has all the answers for upwind and down-wind sails. Shop around! Consider buying second-hand sails for training and only get new ones when you are ready to race.

How many sails to take ?

Take the minimum you think you will require. For instance, if you choose not to take a No 2 it may make a dent in your polar curve when you change from the No 1 to the No 3, but at least you'll be gaining the rest of the time because of the weight saving.

The choice might include:

- Light genoa
- Heavy genoa
- No 2
- No 3
- No 4
- Storm jib
- Drifter
- High-clewed reacher (jib top)
- Light running spinnaker
- Heavy running spinnaker
- Light reaching spinnaker
- Heavy reaching spinnaker
- Asymmetric (if you expect a lot of reaching)
- Light mainsail (inshore - no reefs)
- Heavy mainsail (offshore - has reefs)

DECK GEAR

Don't be afraid to move things around. Look for problems and simple solutions. For example, it's a pain if the spinnaker halyard kinks before it goes through the block at the foot of the mast. This can seriously slow the hoist. A stainless steel ring, which fits the rope diameter closely, held just above the block with elastic, will sort the kinks before they reach the block.

Similarly a short strop from the stem allows you to attach it to the snapshackle of the genoa halyard while the halyard is still attached to the genoa and in the foil groove. You can then pull the rig forward when sailing downwind. The same strop could also be used to facilitate peels from the asymmetric to a reaching kite.

THE RIG

The main elements of setting up your rig are :

- Having the mast upright in the boat, ie preventing it from leaning towards one gunwale.

- Setting the rake, which is controlled by forestay length.

- Setting the prebend, which on keel-stepped masts is controlled, in part, by the relationship between the

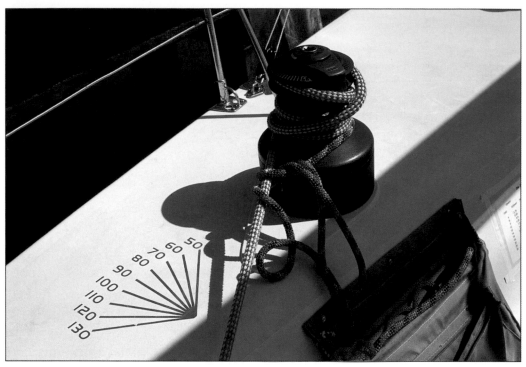

Sighting lines on the deck to help the Tactician/Navigator find the laylines.

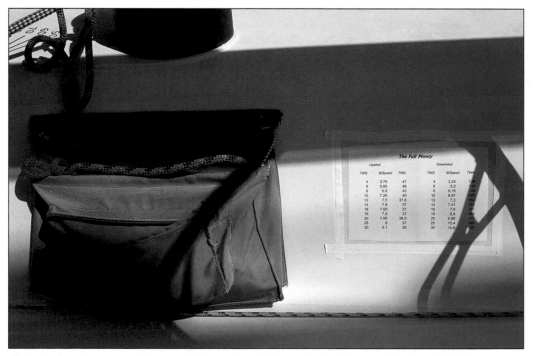

Expected performances figures for upwind and downwind sailing are displayed clearly in the cockpit.

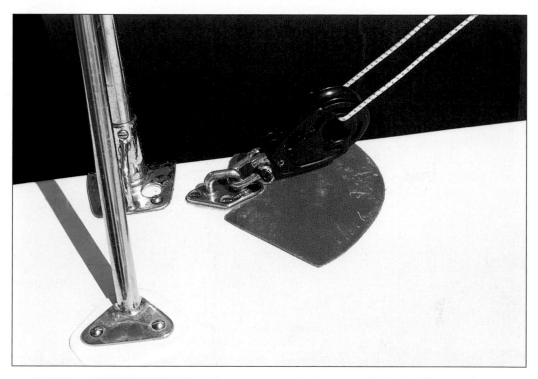

Kevlar pads protect the deck where damage might occur from blocks or the spinnaker pole end.

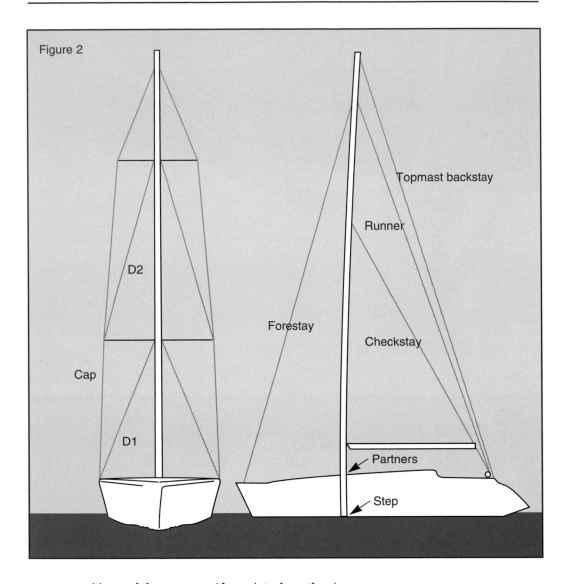

Figure 2

step position and the partners (the point where the rig
passes through the deck). On a deck-stepped mast the
prebend is controlled by the rigging.

• Setting the tension without affecting the above.

Many one designs have known figures for the rig set up.
These are base figures, such as forestay length, from which
to begin the process of finding out what is fast. Get these
from your sailmaker or the designer. Then:

• Step the mast with the rigging loose.

You can achieve pre-bend by chocking the mast forward at the partners (above left), or back at the heel (above right). Sight up the mast to view the pre-bend (left), but measure it by taking the main halyard to the gooseneck and recording the maximum gap.

- Check that the top of the mast is in the middle of the boat by running a halyard down to the port chainplate, then to the starboard one. Look for any difference, then eliminate it.

- Make sure the D's are slack as these will become tighter as you tension the cap shrouds.

- Tension the caps evenly to keep the masthead in the middle.

- Tighten the Ds to keep the mast in column - sight up
  the track.

- Ensure the mast has the right prebend, both in terms of
  amount and position. Your sailmaker will have cut your
  mainsail for a given amount and position of prebend.
  Measure it by drawing the main halyard tight down the
  back of the mast and measuring the distance and position
  of the point of maximum chord.

Now go sailing. Is the leeward shroud too loose?
Does the mast stay in column?

- Make small measured adjustments to correct
  any deviation.

- If the top of the mast is falling off to leeward, the
  D2s may be too tight or the caps may be too loose.
  It's a matter of trial and error.

- If the top of the mast moves to weather, the D1s may
  be too slack or the caps too tight.

PREBEND

With swept aft spreaders, tightening the caps bends the
mast. This is controlled with the D1s or the checkstays.
Prebend allows you to control the shape of the mainsail and
go through the gears. With the checkstays off, the mast
bends and the mainsail is flat. Pull on the checkstays and
the mast straightens, putting more shape in the mainsail.
Indeed, the mainsail is cut for a certain prebend - ask your
sailmaker what it needs. Note that a correctly prebent mast
is safer than a straight one, particularly with the spinnaker
pole pressing aft.

Having got it right, don't throw it all away at the end of the
season - measure the rig set up and record it before you
take everything to pieces.

RAKE

The rake is controlled by the length of the forestay. If, when
sailing upwind, you have too much weather helm then you
want to decrease rake. Conversely, if the helm is light and
lacks feel then you have too little rake. In general, your boat

This Farr 50 has lowers, D1s, D2s, D3s, D4s and jumpers.

*With the rig set up, we're
ready to do battle.*

will go better upwind with more rake and better downwind
with less rake.

On most fractionally rigged boats this is not a big problem,
as upwind rake is maintained by running backstay tension
opposing the forestay length. Downwind the rig can be
drawn forward by easing the backstay and supporting the
mast on a tensioned genoa halyard.

On a masthead rigged boat one has to settle for a
compromise which best suits the race course on the day, as
it is not possible to make such profound changes underway.

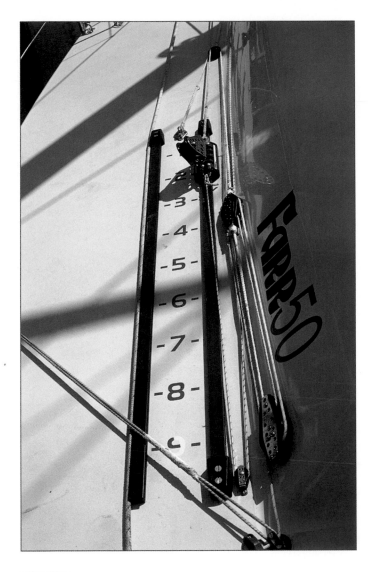

The inboard and outboard genoa tracks are well marked.

TRIM

Provide the Trimmers with lots of visual aids for reference:
telltales, camber stripes, spreader marks, car positions,
marks on sheets and halyards, vision windows in the sails.
All these will help you repeat fast settings.

In training, try lots of sail shapes to see how much each
control needs altering to give a significant change.
Is it 1 cm on the halyard or 30 cm?

The backstay not only controls the mainsail, it affects the

The camber stripes, marked at 50%, are used to gauge the overall depth of the sail. Alter this with the halyard or cunningham: the maximum depth should be about 45% back from the mast.

The cunningham and outhaul are two important controls affecting sail shape. The outhaul controls the camber in the lowest third of the mainsail. Upwind it's pretty tight, and tighter still as the wind increases.

The twist in the leech, shown by the leech telltales, is controlled by the vang, the mainsheet and the traveller.

The black art of genoa trimming.
Firstly, set the runner to give the correct depth to the sail: more runner = flatter sail.
Secondly, adjust the halyard to set the position of the camber: more halyard = camber forward.
Finally, set the twist by a combination of sheet and car adjustments: car back = more twist.
The genoa sheet mainly controls angle of attack: upwind, pull it in to give a good position close to the spreaders.
A good Trimmer continually refers back to the Helm: if height is required flatten the sail, if more power is needed go for more shape.

forestay sag too - so both Mainsail and Genoa Trimmers need to be involved when it is altered. The Mainsheet Trimmer and the Helm need a particular synergy - the mainsheet is helping to steer the boat.

All the crew should be encouraged to communicate relevant information to those who can best use it. For instance, whoever is manning mainsheet and whoever is trimming the genoa should have a constant line of communication running to and from the Helm. Only with a continuous stream of information and feedback will this crucial area of the boat work effectively.

Basically you only need to trim when something changes: the idea is to maintain fast sail shapes and angles in a complex and dynamic environment. It's relatively simple but requires a high level of concentration to maintain the optimum trim hour after hour on the race course.

In particular, you can make good gains in lulls by putting the power on. Ease the genoa sheet, let off the backstay and pull up the traveller. The Helm should be seeking a constant angle of heel by a combination of good sail trimming and steering to give the right angle of attack. The crew can also help here. When the breeze is on, the crew should be on the rail, heads out and hiking hard but in the lulls heads should automatically come in and backsides should move towards the centreline to help maintain the correct angle of heel and feel in the helm.

You can't afford someone's weight to leeward to trim the genoa sheet all the time, so you must fine tune on the mainsheet.

There are lots of tips and tactics to make each and every boat go a little faster than the competition. The list is endless and could almost provide the subject for another book. What cannot be stressed too strongly is the importance of maintaining good trim at all times. Just watch at mark roundings and you will see the boats that find optimum trim fastest after the rounding will gain many boat lengths on their rivals.

Trim, trim, trim and then trim again!

6 Racing around the cans

Around the cans racing is simply the most intense way to learn to race successfully, and most top skippers have spent time racing around the buoys. The skills that can be learned here will improve your chances of victory in every type of racing.

Perhaps predictably, preparation is the foundation of success. A well-prepared boat and crew will nearly always do better on the race course. In order to get the best result possible you will need to have covered at least the basics.

Having sailed on lots of different boats including charter yachts, I have built up a kitbag of basic tools that help prepare any boat for racing. The best boats I have sailed on have this gear readily available and my bag can be left in the car.

Suggested items would definitely include :

- Tape: electrical, duct and self-amalgamating
- Pliers
- Knife
- Bow strop
- Peeling shackles
- Magic marker
- Chart of the racing marks
- Tide tables/tidal atlas
- Stick-on telltales
- Silicon spray (for the luff groove and zips)
- WD40
- Sticky Dacron / spray glue

You will also need a set of sailing instructions and an up-to-date weather forecast.

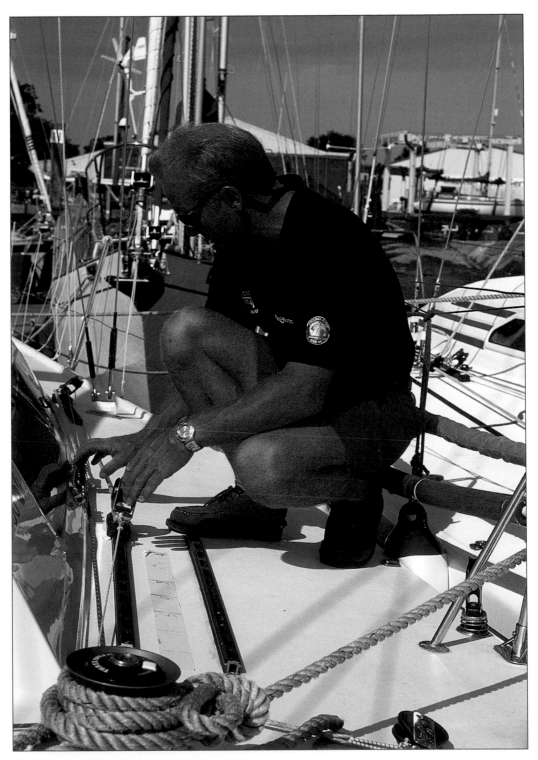

Check everything when you arrive on a new boat.

Next, have a quick check of the boat. Does she have:

- Correct flags
- At least the safety equipment detailed
  in the sailing instructions
- Tools
- Fuel
- Water
- Food
- Charts
- The right sails (see Chapter 5)

There is nothing worse than arriving out at the start area to find you haven't brought something vital. It's a bad start even before the gun has gone!

QUICK FIXES

Here are a few things that will help any boat perform better :

- Remove surplus gear from the boat
- Stow remaining gear in the most appropriate places,
  eg anchor and chain off the bow
- Check the condition of control lines and deck gear
- Check or install outboard leads or barber haulers
- Label everything using a magic marker
- Set up the rig so the mast is in the middle of the boat,
  in column and the rigging is correctly tensioned
- Ensure the instruments and wind gear are
  working properly.

Now at least the boat is workable and you're ready
to go sailing.

ON THE WATER

Hoist the mainsail to its maximum height, then use the downhaul and cunningham to pull the head down to the black band - there is always some stretch in the halyard. Put a mark on the halyard so the Pit has a reference point to hoist to. Fine tuning can be done later.

Now mark all the principal sail controls :

- Genoa halyard at its fully up position. Also mark the
  genoa halyard for the limit of safety when using it to

Mark all the settings.

  pull the rig forward going downwind.
- Mid-positions for the genoa sheet cars
  for all the headsails.
- Position of the wheel when the boat runs straight
  - use this mark to check on weather helm.

Finally, make sure all the instruments work properly and
assess their accuracy.

INITIAL TUNE

For a rookie crew set up the rig so it's easy to use - ie with
a broad groove. For example, in light airs we know it's
fastest to have the draft of the sails at 50% and a tight
headstay - but not many people can sail to that. So go for
a softer entry with a bit of sag in the forestay and move
the draft further forward.

At this level (perhaps at any level) it's not about achieving
excellence all the time; it's about being better than average

most of the time. Good sailors 'change gear' when the
conditions alter. Fine, but beware of being in a constant
state of flux. Your marks will help you when you get
confused, as you can then automatically set up the boat
for medium conditions.

With this philosophy and a couple of hours practise you will
be on your way to being better than most in a straight line.
However, it's the corners that really separate the men from
the boys.

MANOEUVRES

Manoeuvres may represent only 5% of the time on the
water, but doing them right has a major impact on your
performance on the race course. So it's well worthwhile
taking a good deal of time in your training to improve speed
and accuracy in your turns. As skipper, it's your job to make
sure they go right. You yourself must know every
manoeuvre inside out, and understand everyone's job and
the timing.

Your manoeuvres should :

• Be fast
• Be smooth
• Minimise risk to the boat and the crew, ie be in control
• Enable the yacht to exit with speed and accelerate
  up to target speed as quickly as possible

Let's now have a look at the basic racing manoeuvres.

1 Starting

Good results depend on getting a good start. A typical
check list before the start of any yacht race looks like this:

• Monitor the wind from the time you leave the dock.
• Do some sailing and manoeuvres before you get to
  the start area.
• Experiment with various sail configurations.
  Often it's hard to choose between two; if possible,
  test against another boat or watch another pair of
  similar boats tuning up.
• Once you're satisfied, drop the genoa, bag all the sails
  and tidy up. There should be nothing on the foredeck

(you don't want to give away your sail choice) and this leaves you flexible to swap to another genoa if the wind alters just before the start.

- Arrive at the start area in plenty of time
- During the last 20 minutes continue to monitor windshifts and wind trends.
- Check the current against the start marks.
- Take transits from beyond each end of the line. This also gives an opportunity to work with the Bow and check the line from their point of view.
- For a windward start, sail down the line letting out the boom until the mainsail luff just starts to stall (remember, you have no genoa set). Lock off the mainsheet and leave it locked. Tack and sail down the line the other way. If the mainsail stalls more, you are heading towards the favoured end; if it stalls less you are sailing away from the favoured end. Note that this method allows for both wind and tide, and assumes you can't lay the first mark in one.

HITTING THE LINE ON TIME AND IN THE RIGHT PLACE

Modern light boats accelerate well, so timed runs have become far less common. Your objective is to keep close to the line by feathering and easing sheets, then accelerate at the appropriate moment before the gun. You must know how long it takes to get going - a Mumm 36, for example, needs about 30 seconds to get to full speed from a standing start.

You'll also need room to leeward during those final moments to bear way and accelerate. Modern boats won't point unless they've got speed so it's hopeless to go straight onto the wind from rest. Be brave and sail low initially to get boatspeed and activate the lift from your foils.

If you are in a small boat in a mixed fleet it will nearly always pay to start to leeward of larger and faster yachts. This initially seems wrong until you realise that the larger boats will sail faster and climb to windward faster, both clearing your air and keeping other yachts clear. This gives you a clear lane for the first beat. If you do start to windward the yacht will certainly climb over you, necessitating an early tack to clear your air.

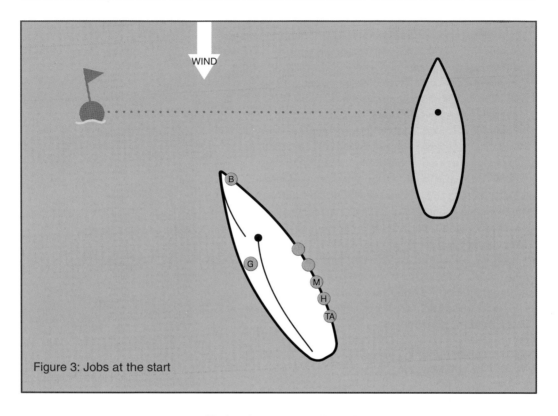

Figure 3: Jobs at the start

Obviously you want clear air at all costs. Be prepared to tack onto port to get it. Remember that when you cross a boat's stern on port you are actually level, because they will have to tack twice to your once (if the mark is to port and you're not laying) and later you're going to be on starboard.

WHAT'S EVERYONE DOING AT THE START?

All the following have their eyes out of the boat.

The Bow (B) is at the forestay, sighting the line and using hand signals to communicate with the cockpit eg five fingers for five boatlengths to the line, hand up or down to indicate 'keep going' or 'slow down'. You naturally want to start ahead of the boats immediately around you, as well as finding a clear lane. If there is a sag in the line-up of other starters the Bow will be able to see it and can call you forward. It's worth remembering that if they can't see the committee boat because of other starters the committee can't see you, so you should be clear!

The Tactician (TA) counts down and monitors the instruments. The Tactician also watchs the other boats and communicates tactical options to the Skipper and Helm (H).

The Mainsheet Trimmer (M) uses the sheet as an accelerator/decelerator, liaising with the Helm who is luffing to slow when necessary but aiming to hit the line on time, with speed and (perhaps most important) in a good clear slot for the first beat.

The Genoa Trimmer (G) also plays the genoa sheet. As the boat comes up to the line they trim on, helping the boat to accelerate to full speed. When trimmed they can get on the rail with everyone else and hike hard as the boat hits the line.

This is a time for maximum effort - everyone on the rail must hike as hard as possible. The focus for the Trimmers and Helm must be to out-accelerate the boats around. If at this point you can just get and hold your nose in front of those around you it will set you on the right course to win.

In all this try not to get too involved with the boat next door - the idea is to get away from people and keep looking at the big picture.

2 Upwind

TACKING

Your objectives for each tack are:

- Speed
- Smoothness
- To re-establish weight on the rail as quickly as possible
- To slow as little as possible, and get back to target speed quickly

Everyone is in position on the rail (Figure 4). The Tactician (TA) calls the tack. The Helm (H) gives the "Ready to tack?" signal, then watches the waves to find a flat area to help smooth the turn, perhaps telling the crew "Hang on, I'm looking for the right wave - OK, tacking".

The Genoa Trimmer (G) is furthest aft in the line-up on the rail. They move to leeward, ready to sheet on the genoa (if

Starting

1. *Here, we're jilling about pre-start, watching the other boats, the breeze, the tide, the line and sizing up the first leg.*

2. *Control the speed of approach to the line by communicating with the trimmers. As a rule slow down by dumping the mainsheet – keep the genoa in a near set position.*

3. *In the last few seconds you should be within a few boatlengths of the line so you can accelerate to cross the line at maximum speed.*

4. *A big hike helps accelerate the boat away from the line.*

1. *Signals from the foredeck. The Bow indicates three boatlengths to go....*

2. *....then two....*

3. *....then one, on the line....*

4. *...Thumbs down would mean we're over.*

there is any slack in the sheet) as the boat heads into the tack. They then wait for the bows to pass through the breeze and let the sheet go at the critical moment - too early and you lose speed, too late and the genoa may end up with a spreader holing the leech. The let-off is a vital part of a good tack and should be practised hard as it affects not only the speed of the sail crossing the fore triangle but the feel of the helm through the tack. It's vital to be able to repeat this part of the process accurately every time. Finally, the Trimmer crosses the boat, taking over from the crew member (W) who has rough-trimmed the genoa and finishes the job of trimming the sail on the new heading - slowly at first, to encourage the boat to accelerate.

The Bow (B) crosses forward of the mast and helps the genoa across if required, lifting the skirt of the sail clear of the rail as the Trimmers bring it on.

The Runner (R) prepares the new runner and brings it on through the tack, easing off the old runner at the same time (if the Helm cannot reach it). The runner, like the genoa, can be brought up slowly to help the boat accelerate. Finally the

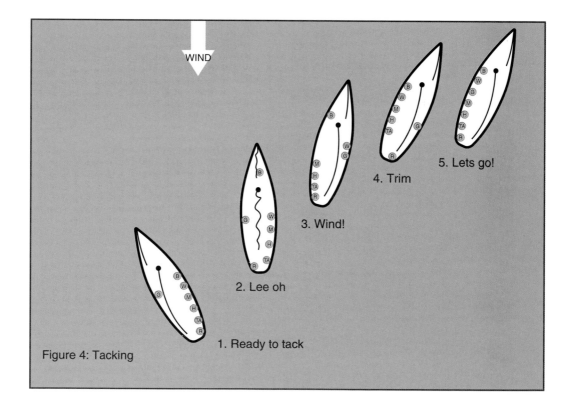

WIND

5. Lets go!

4. Trim

3. Wind!

2. Lee oh

1. Ready to tack

Figure 4: Tacking

1. *'Prepare to tack'. One man drops down to prepare the new runner and let off the genoa sheet. Everyone else remains hiking until the last possible moment.*

2. *'Tacking'. The genoa sheet is let off as the helm is put down. The crew move across the boat smartly on pre-determined routes.*

3. *The Bow helps the genoa around the front of the mast. The new runner is brought on and a call of 'safe' made to the Mainsheet so they know they can now release the leeward runner.*

4. *The genoa is trimmed on and the crew hike out to help the boat accelerate to her optimum upwind speed.*

lazy runner should be prepared for the next tack without locking it off as this might prevent the mainsail from being dumped and could even cause the mast to invert should the mainsheet be released for any reason.

The Mainsheet Trimmer (M) can help by pulling in on the fine tune as the boat goes into the tack, and freeing off afterwards to help the boat accelerate quickly to target speed.

In the midst of all this someone, probably the Tactician, should be calling the boatspeed: "7, 4.5, 5, 6, 7". This gives an idea where you bottomed out and how you're progressing towards the new target speed. If you keep doing this every time, you and your crew will soon start to see an improvement in acceleration and you will also be able to differentiate between a good and a bad tack.

A 'Grand Prix' crew integrate their tacks perfectly - when you do it right you'll know it's right.

CHANGING THE HEADSAIL

If you've had limited practice, then an inside hoist or even a bareheaded change is the easiest. During the Fastnet Race on the Mumm 36 *Group 4*, we often changed bareheaded if it was windy and where the opportunity for a foul-up was too great. We couldn't afford to trash any of our precious sails.

The choice of method will be determined by which slot in the foil the sail is plugged into and, if it's the outboard slot that the new sail must go into, how easy it will be for the crew to raise the new sail behind the old. Often it is very hard to get the sail under the tack of the set genoa, it's a choice! Perhaps a bareheaded change would be quicker.

Headsail changing is all about preparation. Rig a changing sheet either through the same car or another car if that is what the new sail demands. Make sure the second genoa halyard is ready. Your objective is to take the fewest people off the rail. Plug in the new headsail, hoist it and sheet it on.

Blow off the old halyard and drag the old genoa through the gap beneath the new sail and the deck. You will probably need two people to do this. Prevent it sticking by easing the sheet and possibly luffing slightly.

REEFING THE MAINSAIL

Most boats don't like to be overpressed. Reefing at the right time will improve your speed dramatically. Build up your sail change diagram to show accurately the wind speeds at which to make the changes. If you are going to windward it will generally pay to change down headsails first, because the mainsail helps you achieve height.

'Grand Prix' boats seldom reef, many don't even have the facility built into their sails. They manage without a reef by blading out the mainsail:

- Increase prebend by easing off the checkstay
- Tension the outhaul
- Tension the cunningham
- Tension the runner
- Tension the backstay

If you do need a reef then ensure that it goes in snugly. Correct pennant position and good halyard tension are crucial for a good shape. These can still be adjusted to control the shape of the mainsail and don't necessarily need to be barred up tight. Again it's about changing gears to suit conditions. In heavy weather it's important to take care to reef well; always assume the weather will worsen.

UPWIND TIPS

Look ahead and communicate

To you it may be obvious what's going to happen, but don't assume it's obvious to the crew. Look ahead and decide which manoeuvres will be required. Then tell everyone your intentions: "We'll do two more tacks, then come in to the mark on starboard. It'll be a bear away set, with starboard pole".

Don't worry that your plan may change - issue an 'update' as things develop: "No need to tack, the tide's sweeping us up to the mark. Still a bear-away set".

Don't attempt something unachievable.

You may want to luff hard, gybe, hoist the genoa, drop the kite, gybe again and round the leeward mark perfectly, but

A tack change.

1. *The Bow organises a halyard.*

2. *The headsail is passed forward. It has been organised properly with the tack shown by the arrow on the bag.*

3. *The halyard is fixed on and the sail slid into the luff groove.*

6. *The boat is tacked.*

7. *The old sail is lowered inside the new genoa.*

in 50 yards it's almost certain to be a foul-up.
Remember KISS: Keep It Simple Stupid.

Look a long way ahead

At the beginning of each leg think where you want to be
at the end, and how you will approach the mark. On a
beat, for example, 75% of the fleet will come in on
starboard, so it may pay to come in on port, planning to
slot in early enough to get the kite ready. But don't
forget KISS.

4. *The trimmer takes the starboard*   **5.** *The new sail is hoisted.*
genoa sheet and attaches it to the new sail.

8,9. *It is sorted out and bagged on the windward deck.*

3 Downwind

HOISTING THE SPINNAKER

Let's look now at a simple spinnaker hoist - the bear-away set. Other options are given in Fernhurst's companion volume *Racing Crew* by Malcolm McKeag.

- If the next leg is borderline for the spinnaker, don't be in a rush to hoist. You won't lose too much ground if you white sail reach until you are sure that a kite is right.

- Tell the Bow your plan, so they can set up the gear.

- A primary consideration is to keep the weight on the rail as long as possible during the approach to the mark. Only the Bow should be off the rail clipping the kite gear together.

- Then if required the Mast and Pit can come in and help set the pole in the final few metres.

A bear-away set. Raise the pole as you approach the mark.

The pole is up and set. The Bow clips on the spinnaker.

Sneak the guy up to the pole end on the final approach.

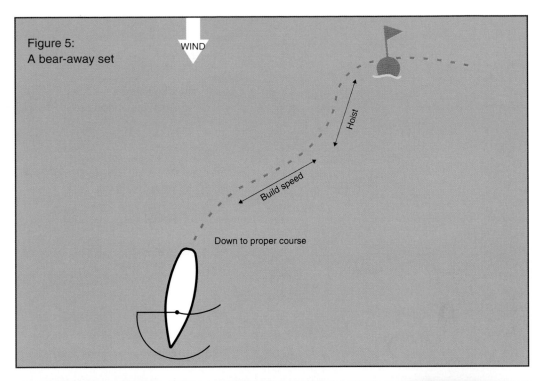

Figure 5:
A bear-away set

WIND

Hoist

Build speed

Down to proper course

Begin the hoist.

Bear away around the mark. The Trimmers work on getting the kite to set.

With the kite set, drop the headsail immediately.

When things go wrong... a typical hourglass   *Pull down onto the clew to encourage the spinnaker to open. No go!*

- Help the turn by easing the mainsheet. This helps the boat to bear away without using an excessive amount of helm. Also ease the genoa, maintaining fast trim through the turn.

- Make sure the guy and sheet are loaded onto their winches.

- Don't call the hoist until you're heading downwind.

- Meanwhile sneak the tack back to the pole by pulling on the guy. Stop when the pole is just off the forestay.

- The Pit and Mast hoist and the Bow feeds the sail out of the bag.

Lower the halyard, which will further encourage the sail to open. If neccessary, lower until the crew can reach the problem.

Then re-hoist.

- The action on the sheet is now critical. Compromise between sheeting on late (which may let the sail twist and form a wineglass) and sheeting too much and too soon (which prevents the twist, by separating the clews, but fills the sail early and possibly leads to a broach).

- When the spinnaker fills it is nearly always oversheeted, so ease out the sheet quickly to get it to fly properly and maintain control.

- Once the spinnaker is hoisted the Pit blows the headsail halyard and the Bow gathers in. The kite probably won't fill properly until the headsail is down.

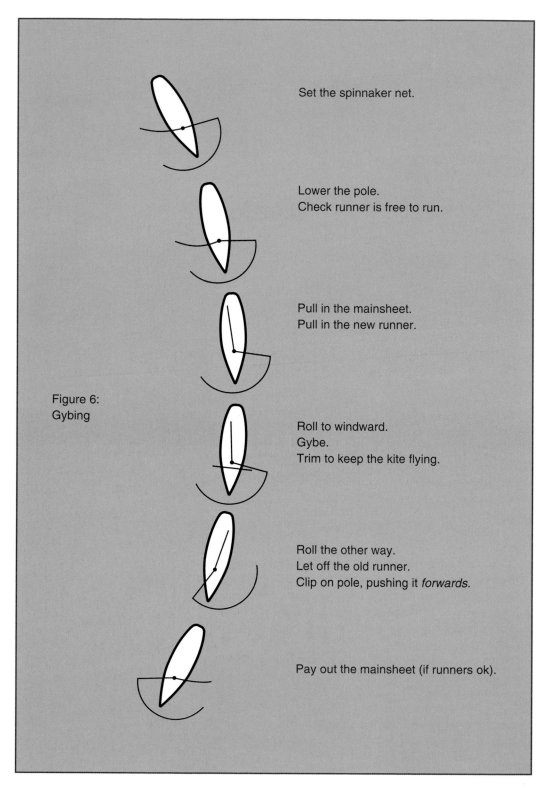

Set the spinnaker net.

Lower the pole.
Check runner is free to run.

Pull in the mainsheet.
Pull in the new runner.

Figure 6:
Gybing

Roll to windward.
Gybe.
Trim to keep the kite flying.

Roll the other way.
Let off the old runner.
Clip on pole, pushing it *forwards*.

Pay out the mainsheet (if runners ok).

GYBING THE SPINNAKER

The spinnaker is a powerful sail and many crews find it more daunting than using other sails. Gybing practice and clear job allocation will reduce the crew's fears. Nothing is more satisfying than getting this one right.

Good gybing is just a question of practice. Practise until you can get it right under pressure: it's no good doing your dummy runs in a clear bit of water. You need to be able to throw in a gybe and be confident that the crew can handle it. So head for a buoy, gybe and then repeat, reducing the distance to go until the team can do it quickly and easily. Treat any problems as part of the training - after all, things will go wrong on the race course.

There is much to be said for trying different gybing options. Some Bows prefer 'end for ending' while others prefer 'dip poling'. Whatever the Bow's preference, go with what is fast and reliable and use your training to increase confidence if the chosen technique is not the preferred technique. Having a broad repertoire is an important part of any good crew's skills.

On today's high performance boats it's important to gybe with pace if you are to stand any chance of coming out of the gybe with speed and, in stronger conditions, with the boat on it's feet. Also, if you allow the boat to slow down the apparent wind increases and everything loads up, making the job much harder. So practise getting through the gybe quickly.

Despite this, it's important to keep the kite flying throughout the manoeuvre and this is the job of the Trimmers and Helm. It's a common mistake to place too much importance on the pole - if it's off for a while it simply doesn't matter. Indeed it is a good thing to practise without a pole (this also has the benefit of leading on to a float drop). On many boats it is possible for someone to hold out the tack of the spinnaker, effectively becoming a human pole, while you are performing this exercise.

Prepare to gybe. Head up a few degrees to gain speed. Good speed equals a good gybe.

Begin the turn. Steer away under the kite. Call 'trip'.

Centre the main. Often it's wo₁ holding it centred to help the spinnaker fly through the gybe Change the runners. "Gybing

ROLES THROUGH THE GYBE

Helm

The Helm should gybe as the boat rolls to windward, and call the trip at the apex of the roll (ie when the roll is at the maximum angle). This gives the least weight on the guy and also helps the boat bear away into the turn with minimum rudder. Then, as the boat rolls the other way, the kite will automatically move over onto the new side and into clear air. Now is the time for the pole to be clipped onto the new guy - if the Bow misses they may have to wait until the spinnaker has rolled out to windward again. The Helm can help the Bow a great deal by steering under the kite to achieve this.

Above all, don't panic and don't shout: the crew will appreciate this. Bear in mind that you are losing very little in having the pole unclipped for a few seconds.

The lazy guy is clipped into the new pole end and the pole pushed out and forward. Check the new runner is on, then pay out the main.

The pole is clipped back onto the mast. Head up a few degrees to regain speed.

Set up on the new gybe and steer to maintain optimum downwind speed.

Mainsheet

At the beginning of the gybe, the Mainsheet Trimmer should pull in on the mainsheet until the boom is over the boat. It often helps the kite to stay full, at the apex of the gybe, if the Mainsheet holds the boom on the centreline for a few seconds after the gybe is completed. In larger boats you can't afford to crash-gybe the boom across the boat. The risk is that you break either the boom and/or the gooseneck, as well as being marginally out of control for the few seconds the boom is sweeping across the deck. It's really about maintaining control of the mainsail throughout the gybe.

The Mainsheet Trimmer needs to work with the crew member(s) controlling the runners. It is important to watch carefully and if there's no-one on the leeward runner hold on before paying out the mainsheet. If there is a mistake on the runner, it will be the Mainsheet who drops the rig! Should a mistake occur, the leach of the mainsail will hold the spar up while the problem is rectified.

Trimmers

The Trimmers' job is to keep the kite full through the gybe. The trick is to trim the kite around the forestay at the same rate as the Helm turns the boat. To do this, the Trimmers must watch both the sail and the horizon and work in unison to judge the turn. On a small boat, one person can do this job by standing in the middle of the boat and controlling both sheets.

It's a common mistake to strap the kite into the boat. This is very likely to cause a wrap and, in any case, is not fast. It is far better to get the sail as far in front of the boat as possible while maintaining control.

Bow

Try to make sure the Bow has time to get everything set up. They may need to lower the inboard end of the pole temporarily by sliding it down the mast to make an 'end for end' gybe easier or raise it to make a 'dip pole' gybe easier.

On most small to medium sized yachts, 'end for ending' the pole seems to offer the most control and speed but with 'end for ending' the main difficulty is getting the pole back on after the gybe. The trick here is to clip the pole onto the guy and push it out forwards towards the spinnaker clew, not out sideways as seems more natural.

Pit

The Pit may have to help the Bow by easing either uphaul, downhaul or both. Otherwise the Pit can assist the Trimmers by grinding as appropriate.

Runner

The Runner's job in a gybe is of course highly critical. In a strong breeze a small mistake in this area could drop your rig over the front of the boat. Every boat is different but in general pull on the new runner as the mainsheet is brought in. It is surprising how much this can help the Mainsheet Trimmer get the boom over the boat. Prepare the loaded runner for immediate release as the boom crosses the boat. If the runner is left jammed in a self tailer and the mainsail is gybed onto the loaded runner, it is possible that the checkstays, under the additional load of the mainsail, will invert the mast causing a potential breakage.

With the new runner up and loaded, give a call of 'SAFE', letting both the Mainsheet Trimmer and whoever is releasing the old runner know that the rig is now held and they can release their controls.

It is a good idea for the Runner to be able to repeat settings - a change in runner tension will have a profound effect on sail trim. Put marks on the runner tail to indicate when the runner is right. On some boats, forestay load is measured by a load cell in the forestay pin and displayed on the boat's instrumentation for the Runner and Trimmers to see.

DROPPING THE SPINNAKER

Like most sailing manoeuvres there are a variety of methods of achieving a good clean spinnaker drop. These are outlined in *Racing Crew*. Having a good repertoire will provide you with options as the downwind mark closes.

Long before you arrive at the mark make your plan for the drop, the rounding and your set up and positioning for the next leg.

Aim to get the headsail up early and make the drop in plenty of time. A highly skilled crew will be able to leave it later, but if you try this and things go wrong you could lose a lot of ground. So, as with all things, balance risk and reward.

Downwind you will have the mainsail much fuller, with both halyard and outhaul eased. Bring these back on in plenty of time for the next upwind leg. Rounding and heading upwind with these loose will be slow.

The Pit will have flaked out the spinnaker halyard to prevent foul-ups during the drop.

The Bow and Mast will most likely lead the gathering crew.

The smart crew thinks ahead to the next hoist, so these drops give you options on which side the gear ends up. If you do it right, you can leave the sail in the forepeak, and hoist it out of the hatch without repacking.

A leeward drop. Hoist the headsail.

Leave the genoa sheet very loose to prevent the kite collapsing prematurely.

A windward drop. Lose the pole.

"Ready". The Bow takes the (windward) lazy sheet.

*Harden up round the mark.
Blow the halyard.*

*Drop the kite underneath the genoa.
Then trim for the beat.*

*The Bow pulls the sail around the front
of the forestay and down the hatch.*

*Coming up on the breeze for the new wind-
ward leg. A crew member stationed below the
hatch to gather makes this manoeuvre easier.*

On a 35-footer you may need three people, on a 70- footer you may need five.

On the Challenge yacht we generally dropped our spinnaker 'through the letterbox' ie retrieving the sail between the boom and the loose-footed mainsail. On the Mumm 36 we often dropped the sail down the forehatch, leaving it clipped on for the next hoist. This requires a lot of pre-planning on the part of the Bow who needs to know whether to drop the sail to windward, round the front of the forestay (a windward drop) or to leeward round the back of the genoa (a leeward drop). This will depend on which side of the boat the next hoist will occur. Thinking ahead and relaying the information is important here.

Ten boat lengths from the mark begin to sneak up the headsail. At six boat lengths it should be up. When the time comes, the Pit blows the first 2/3rds of the halyard to take the weight out of the sail. Try to prevent the sail going in the water as this is slow and will make the sail heavy for the next set.

Blow the guy just afterwards. The kite will almost lie above the water and can be retrieved easily. While the kite is coming down concentrate on getting everything ready for the beat ahead. The mainsheet will be coming in, the headsail will be getting trimmed on as you round and every effort should be made to hit target numbers quickly. Again everyone who is on the rail should hike out to help the boat accelerate.

Your Bow should work to clear the foredeck, giving the call of "clear to tack" as quickly as possible after the mark. You may need to tack to get into clear air if other boats are around.

As swiftly as possible get the kite repacked and settle everyone down for the beat.

FLOAT DROP

If it is necessary to tack the boat almost immediately after rounding the mark, try a Float Drop. Here the pole is put away early, so you will be clear to tack immediately after the mark. Sail relatively deep towards the mark with a pole-less spinnaker. This can be kept full by a crew member

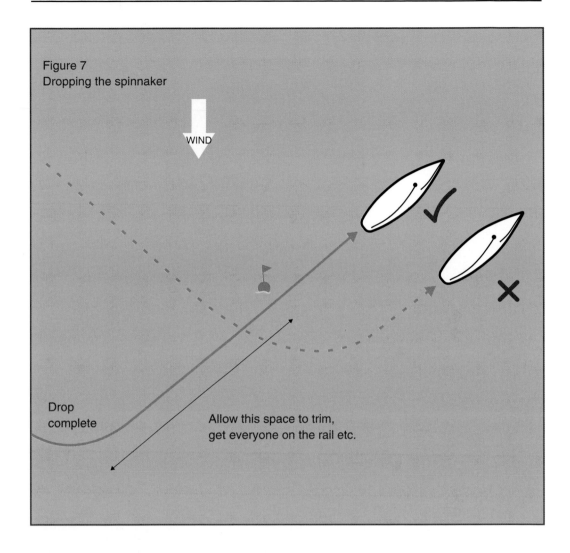

Figure 7
Dropping the spinnaker

WIND

Drop
complete

Allow this space to trim,
get everyone on the rail etc.

pushing out the sheet or guy on the windward side like a
human pole. There is the added advantage of being able to
drop the sail to windward (a windward drop) if required.

DOWNWIND TIPS

Soaking down

Generally while sailing downwind you will sail on the
pressure. What this means is that you will soak down in the
puffs and maintain speed in the lulls by luffing slightly.
Remember the objective is to be the most downwind boat.
If you are, the chances are you will be ahead. The Sheet

A float drop is ideal for a drop followed by a gybe. Use it when approaching on the "wrong" gybe.

1. *Hoist the headsail and get ready.*   **2.** *Trip the pole. A crew member acts as a human g*

4. *Blow the halyard. The kite will normally float away*   **5.** *The kite is still coming down as the boat gybes.*
from the boat, but here there's insufficient breeze.

3. *Put the pole away. Now you're clear to gybe.*

6. *Set up for the next windward leg.*

Trimmer should be constantly calling the pressure in the sail - too much pressure and you are too high and could be getting downwind faster, too little pressure and you will be slow.

Rolling

If the boat is rolling too much, ease the pole forward and down. Pull down on the tweakers if you have them or perhaps use the lazy guy. Tension the vang to stabilise the rolling, but have it manned in case of a broach.

Broaching

Avoid a broach by having someone calling the breeze. Bear away sharply in the gusts, easing the sheet to help the boat stay on its feet. When the gust has passed you can luff up to maintain power.

If you do broach:

- Dump the vang
- Ease the spinnaker sheet
- Pull back the guy
- If the rudder stalls be brave, centre it to get reattachment of flow over the blade, then try again
- If things go badly wrong you may have to take the kite down

NIGHT SAILING

Although night sailing should be no more dangerous than sailing during the day, it's worth commenting on the additional problems it presents the racing skipper.

On the Challenge races many crew members came to me and asked why we did so little training at night. I always replied that in my opinion sailing at night was exactly the same as sailing during the day only with the lights off - I still believe this.

Sailing at night can be very satisfying and is certainly an added challenge. Surfing with 25 knots of breeze and big waves on a moonlit night can be wonderful, provided you are prepared and in control!

You will need good lighting for trimming sails if you are to continue to race as if it were daylight. I am a huge advocate of lighting up any problems we have on deck and am certainly not in the group of racing sailors who believe you should be able to do everything in the dark. The one exception is when you don't want to advertise a sail change or manoeuvre to close rivals. I would train my crew for this but not make it a regular practice.

Remember that if you do light up the boat your night visibility will drop dramatically. Keep a close watch for surrounding boats and obstructions.

You should also be aware that you and your crew will be at a low ebb during the early hours - it's normal biorhythms and your body clock just doing what it always does. Your watch system should take all this into account. If a crew member becomes very tired, get them to bed. They will be a danger to themselves and others and it's far better to have them back in 'working order' as soon as possible.

Prepare for each night sail ensuring :

- Everyone is wearing lifejackets and harnesses
- The crew is well fed and as rested as possible
  (see watch systems)
- The boat is tidy - everything is in its place
- All lights are working - fresh batteries in torches etc
- Hot drinks and snacks are available
  (we always have a large thermos flask)

WATCH SYSTEMS

There are probably as many watch systems as there are skippers. Everyone has their own idea. On the Challenge races we ran a watch system of two six-hour watches during the day and three four-hour watches during the night, with a watch leader on each. This worked well throughout two round the world races and the crews seemed to like it.

On the Mumm 36 *Group 4* we seldom sailed on long races and watch systems were virtually non-existent with nearly everyone except the Helm having to stay on the rail. It really depends on the make-up and strength of the crew, the type of race and the type of boat you are sailing.

WATCH CHANGES

Watch changes need to be well organised all the time, but at night this is even more crucial. On the Challenge our new watch was woken 15 minutes before they were required on deck. This gave them time to dress properly, have a hot drink and generally get their act together before appearing on deck.

As each new watch member comes out of the hatch they should call out to the 'on-deck' crew who they are and that they are now on deck. This allows the 'on-deck' watch leader and their watch to keep track of who is where on the boat. Watch changes can be a dangerous time on a pitch dark night in rough conditions. I don't allow the 'on watch' to come below while the new watch is coming up. Each 'on watch' crew member hands over to his or her opposite number and passes on any and all relevant information.

The Helm passes on course steered, target boatspeed, apparent wind angle, true wind direction together with any trends in either the breeze or sea state. Any navigational or other information about surrounding boats should also be passed on. Before taking the helm the new Helm stands behind the wheel to get a feel for what is happening and, when the change happens the old Helm watches the new Helm to see that they have got the hang of it, offering advice if required. This may seem long-winded but the loss of speed during a helm change can be very damaging. Once the crew is used to the routine, the off-going watch can be down below five or ten minutes after the new watch has

arrived on deck and very little speed has been lost. The
Bow and every other crew member do the same hand-over
process, all seeking a seamless change.

HELMING TECHNIQUE AT NIGHT

With the telltales lit, good instruments and someone
spotting the waves and wind on the water you should, with
practice, be able to sail as well at night as you can during
the day. It's really not possible to explain how to steer
through waves, it's a matter of practice and experience.

In the unlikely event that there is no ambient light, you may
have to sail almost entirely on instruments using either
apparent or true wind angles. This can be very tiring and
Helms will need more regular breaks in these conditions.

Get on course and trim the sail plan accordingly. The Helm
then steers to the sail plan trying to get to target speed.
When the boat is being steered like this the Navigator must
keep a close eye on the course over the ground and
position, to monitor for windshifts or changes in the current.

If, for example, the Helm is heading well above the
required line the Navigator can ask that the sheets be eased
and the process of finding the new target speed is then
repeated. If the Helm is heading below the required line the
sheets should be hardened. In short, the Helm concentrates
on speed and the Navigator concentrates on where the boat
is going.

7 Race navigation

Knowledge is power

'Grand Prix' racers go to extraordinary lengths to get knowledge about the race course. No detail is too small to be worth knowing. There is no limit to the knowledge you can get provided you have enough time and resource. The more clearly you understand the area you are racing in, the more likely you are to have a competitive edge. It's true to say that the sailor sailing in his home waters should have an advantage over any visitor - it's a perfect example of knowledge being power.

The information that will help includes general weather conditions, local wind patterns, tidal streams and geography, both above and below the water. You need to ensure you cover all parts of the race course. I would also be looking for other sources of information available throughout the race, predominantly weather via weather-fax, radio, Internet, satellite or any other legal means. Produce your own schedule of when and where these products are available for the duration of the race.

Having collated as much information as possible, plan out the bare bones of your route and commit this to paper to focus your thoughts. Once afloat, ensure the crew know what your strategy is and use the feedback constructively. Give scenarios based on various wind and tide combinations. When the time comes you may need to modify these plans, but that's much easier than starting from scratch. Obviously you will need to be open about changing your mind.

Your overall strategy will almost certainly need to be modified for tactical considerations. From the moment the gun goes off, the actions of other boats may demand a reaction from you. It's vital to know where the fleet is and where you want to be in relation to the other boats. If the body of the fleet heads left, for example, do you really want to go right? Tactics is all about playing the percentages. A 50/50 chance is not a good gamble. It is far safer to minimise the potential for a disaster.

WEATHER ROUTING

Round the cans races

Having collected the relevant local knowledge and the latest weather information before leaving the dock, it is important to observe continually the cloud formation and changes in the weather patterns while on the race course.

Offshore races

For longer offshore races your localised knowledge and latest weather information will take you so far. After that you will need to utilise your onboard equipment to interpret what is most likely to happen. Weather faxes, broadcasts from coastal radio stations, satellite images and marine products from the Internet (if allowed) will all help, but don't forget to continue to monitor the visual and measurable changes.

Your hourly log entries should include the barometric pressure, wind speed and wind direction, and these together with your own visual observations will help to build up a picture and help you pinpoint exactly where you are within a weather system.

Ocean and round the world races

Weather routing is most frequently associated with this type of longer race. It is now possible to source huge databases of information relatively easily, enabling you to produce very high quality statistical routes before the start.

In its simplest form this means that you can make a reasonable prediction of the predominant weather systems that will affect your route. With this information it is possible to modify the great circle route to provide an optimum course for your boat's polar performance.

In practice what this means is that you can plan waypoints that modify the shortest distance course to give the best possibility of ideal wind strengths and angles. These waypoints are unimportant as points to pass through. They merely emphasise a deviation away from the shortest route, indicating perhaps which side of the fleet to place yourself.

Try to focus on simple rules to help find the best route. If the breeze is set to shift to the right as you face it, you should try to make your way to the right hand side of the fleet. Conversely if the breeze is going left, go left.

Routing around major systems can be made simpler by thinking about how your yacht passes through the concentric circles of the isobars. If you are heading upwind around a depression, the low pressure system will pass to the right of you in the northern hemisphere and to the left in the southern hemisphere. Put simply, you will reach into the system, beat as the system is directly adjacent to you then reach out on the opposite tack.

If you pass closer to the system's centre you will need to spend less time close on the wind than a boat which is sailing further away from the system. This will probably mean a gain. The one disadvantage may be your closer proximity to the more severe weather.

If your route passes around a high it will often pay to do the opposite, staying further away from the system's centre. If the high expands you will be the last to be captured by the lighter airs and the first to be released. Being further away from the centre also means that when the wind drops you will be able to sail higher and pass (hopefully) ahead of rivals closer to the high centre. The one disadvantage is that you will sail through a longer area of directly downwind sailing that could be slower. It's really a matter of studying your yacht's polars and finding the best compromise.

WHAT TO WORK OUT IN ADVANCE

Make sure you take with you full details of tides and currents. Set up waypoints at any headlands, as well as the finish, and ensure you have a note of any prearranged routing waypoints. Carry good charts of any headlands or inshore sections of the course; this is not an area to save either weight or money.

You will need detailed information on weather and if your memory for the sea breeze rules is like mine, carry a copy of *Wind Strategy* by David Houghton. Carrying this excellent book won us a leg of the BT Global Challenge - Sydney to Cape Town. *Concert* was ahead by eight miles with 60 miles to go to Cape Town. I skulked into the heads

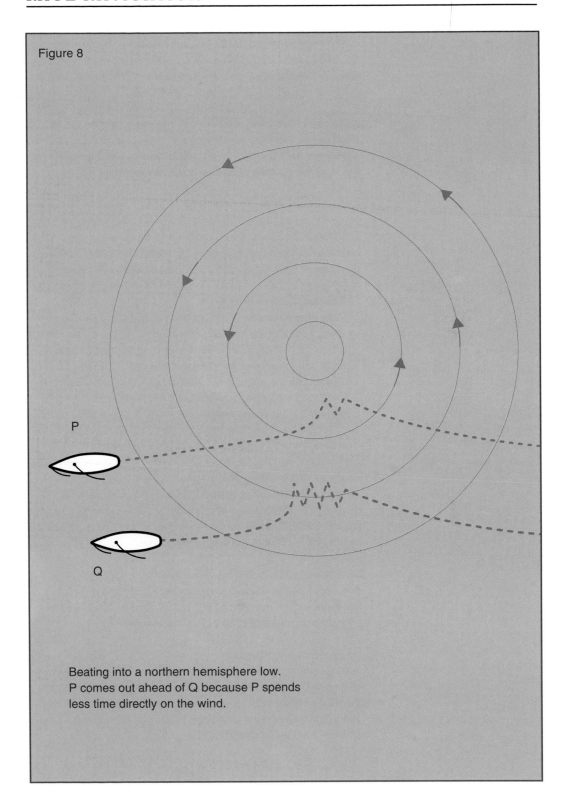

Figure 8

Beating into a northern hemisphere low.
P comes out ahead of Q because P spends
less time directly on the wind.

with a copy of *Wind Strategy* and worked out that we needed to go further inshore to catch the sea breeze as it came in. We headed inshore and still with very little breeze I retired to bed.

Some time later I was woken with the news that we were reaching to the finish in 18 knots of breeze with *Concert* offshore in two knots of wind. It had worked and we won the leg by a quarter of a mile, after racing 8,000 miles!

SAILING AROUND HEADLANDS

The tide is modified dramatically as it flows around a headland, so on coastal legs plan ahead carefully to make best use of each shore feature. Remember :

* Tide turns first inshore.
* Tide runs strongest close to a headland because the water funnels fast past the obstruction. There is, however, a small patch of slack water extending a short distance from the shore (due to frictional effects).
* There may be a back eddy downtide of the headland.
* If there is a bay on either side of the headland the wind will be lighter in the bays.

WAYPOINT CLOSURE

Always keep the final destination in mind while racing offshore. Monitor your speed made good towards your destination - known as VMC (velocity made down the course) or WCV (waypoint closure velocity) - tacking or gybing on each windshift as appropriate.

On a windward leg you must get upwind and on a downwind leg you need to get downwind, but sail on the longest tack or gybe first - unless your weather or navigational research has revealed a faster route.

Often the biggest gains are made as you approach the next mark or the destination. You need to arrive fast, not beating or having to sail too deep. So often the positions change in the final stretch. Boats that positioned themselves well and can sail fast often overtake those that may have led for most of the leg but have not considered the final approach.

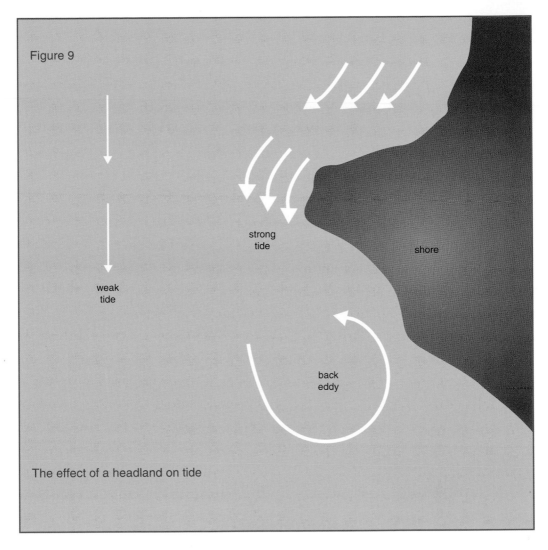

Figure 9

weak
tide

strong
tide

shore

back
eddy

The effect of a headland on tide

KEY POINTS OF NAVIGATION

1. Sail the shortest distance through the water. When boat logs are compared after the race the winner almost always has the lowest reading.

2. Sail near the great circle or rhumb line. Sail the shortest course unless your research has revealed a faster route. Perhaps draw a limiting cone around your course line to limit how far you deviate from the shortest route. A five or ten degree cone should be sufficient, depending on the length of the leg. Once outside this you risk sailing extra distance through the water (contravening the first rule).

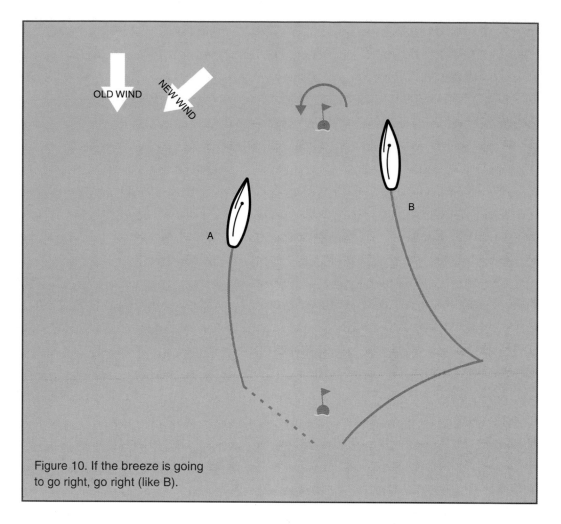

Figure 10. If the breeze is going
to go right, go right (like B).

3. Predict windshifts from the weather map. The wind
seldom stays constant on a long leg. Try to predict which
way the breeze will swing, then head towards the new wind.
If the breeze is going to go right, go right. If the breeze is
going to go left, go left.

In Figure 11 the boat gybes on the shift, staying inside the
'safe' cone and getting a good angle in to the mark.

4. Don't arrive downtide of the next mark. And never
place yourself downtide and downwind of it - beating into
the stream is no fun.

5. Stay on the making tack or gybe. Suppose your boat
sails upwind at 40 degrees to the true wind. If your course is
more than 40 degrees off the mark, you must consider

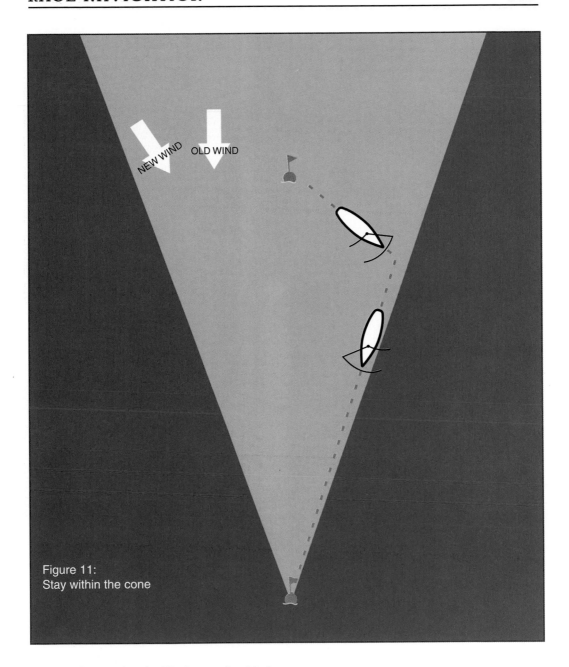

NEW WIND   OLD WIND

Figure 11:
Stay within the cone

tacking. In practice the Navigator should give you a
maximum COG bearing for this to prevent the Helm from
simply following the shift onto a non-making tack.

Suppose however that the wind is varying wildly with shifts
pushing you away from the mark. If the shifts are of
reasonable duration it may pay to tack on a header and

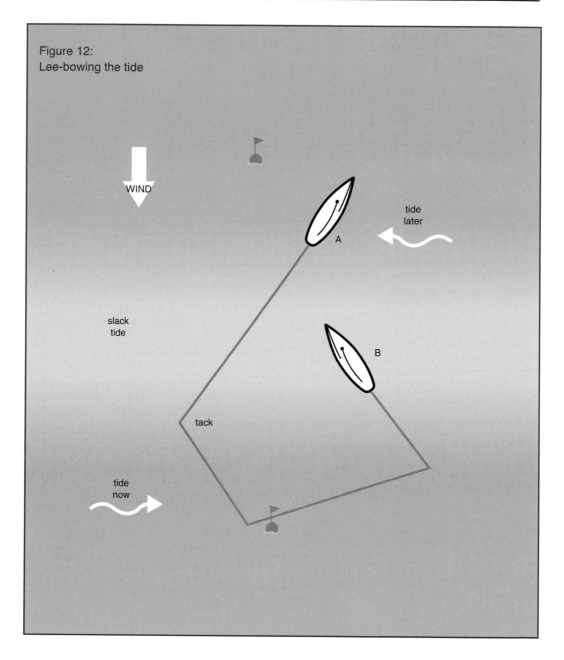

Figure 12:
Lee-bowing the tide

WIND

tide
later

slack
tide

tack

tide
now

A

B

make a gain to windward as each shift comes through. Hard work, but you will make big gains on a boat that simply ends up on a dead beat to the mark at the end.

6. Tack on the tide. If you are beating into a cross-tide, aim to keep the tide under your lee bow. Boat A in Figure 12 sets off on starboard, tacks onto port as the tide turns and is

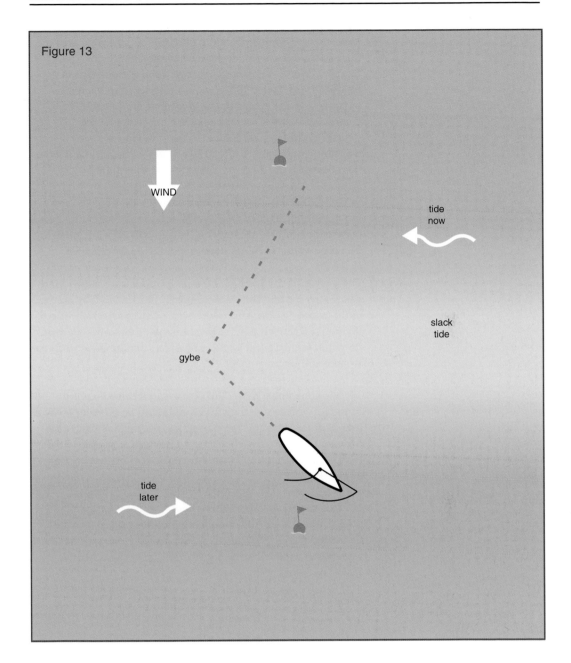

Figure 13

pushed upwind by the tide on both tacks. To be safe she should, in fact, tack before the tide turns to make sure she arrives up-tide of the next mark (see rule 4). Boat B does the opposite, and loses out.

7. Gybe on the tide. The boat in Figure 13 increases her apparent wind by choosing her gybe to match the tide.

8. Beware of land masses. It is essential that you carry all the relevant charts, pilots and tidal information for your intended route and any diversions/refuge ports that may be necessary. Listen to the local radio forecast as you approach. If you are racing to a foreign shore try to have someone on board who speaks the language. If, for example, the forecast indicates that the land will be warming you might reasonably expect a sea breeze during the afternoon or drainage breeze later that night.

9. Consider speed differences later in the leg. Let's say the passage in Figure 14 is estimated to take six hours at our current speed of eight knots. So there will be a net westerly tide for two hours. What course should we steer as we leave A?

The answer is to lay off to the east immediately. If the wind decreases we will slow down, spend more than four hours in the westerly tide, and need every yard gained up-tide of the mark. If the wind increases, on the other hand, we won't go much faster (eight knots is near our maximum speed) so we will still be on course.

10. Monitor your WCV/VMC. Having worked out the optimum course you may find that luffing or bearing away a few degrees gives more speed; maybe you can catch the waves better, or hoist the kite. Do beware, however, of a temporary gain putting you downtide or downwind of the next mark.

11. Sail the fleet. If the whole fleet has just disappeared to the left and you're still steadfastly heading right, double and triple check your strategy. Surely they can't all be wrong. Perhaps it's time to cover and play the odds.

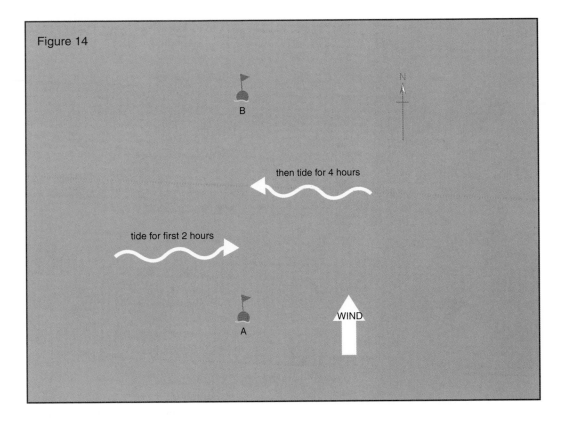

Figure 14

12. Never hesitate to call the Navigator. Often you have a gut feeling that there is going to be a change in the weather, the wind or the tide. Cocooned in electronic gadgetry, the Navigator may have missed the signs. Wake him and ask him to rework his calculations until you are sure you are going the right way.

Figure 15 shows how these rules can be applied to various combinations of wind and tide. In each case the yacht is sailing from X to Y.

Sailing from X to Y offshore	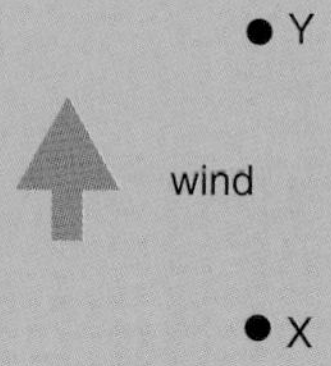 Dead Run	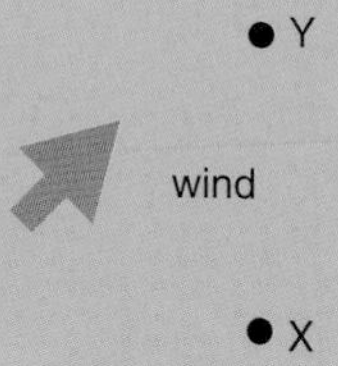 Broad Reach
No Tide	1 Tack downwind at the fastest angle.	7 Sail rhumb line.
Wind Expected To Veer	2 If large veer expected soon, set off on port. If small veer expected later, set off on starboard and gybe on the shift.	8 Small veer - sail straight. Large veer - luff a little.
Wind Expected To Back	3 Opposite to (2).	9 Begin on port, gybe on the shift.
Tide To Right	4 Start on port gybe in case wind drops later. If the tide will turn during the leg, set off on starboard then gybe on the tide.	10 Steer the heading required for rhumb line course.
Following Tide	5 As (1).	11 As (10).
Adverse Tide	6 As (1).	12 As (10).

Figure 15

● Y → wind ● X **Reach** (just too close to spinnaker)	● Y ↘ wind ● X **Close Reach**	● Y ↓ wind ● X **One-Sided Beat**	● Y ↓ wind ● X **Beat**
13 Set kite and bear off. Drop kite later and close reach up to mark.	19 Sail rhumb line.	25 Sail the long leg first.	31 Keep within the 'funnel' and play the windshifts.
14 Luff early.	20 Luff as high as possible. After veer stay on port until this becomes losing tack - then tack .	26 Keep on port. Tack when starboard becomes the making tack.	32 Port tack, starboard after shift.
15 Put kite up now and bear off.	21 Sail straight and prepare to set the kite.	27 Port tack.	33 Starboard tack, port after shift.
16 Danger of being swept downtide. Luff onto close reach; set kite later.	22 Steer the heading required for rhumb line course.	28 Port tack.	34 Starboard tack (takes you closer to mark).
17 As (13) but drop kite early.	23 Sail straight.	29 Port tack.	35 As (31). Beware of overstanding.
18 As (13) but drop kite late.	24 Sail straight.	30 Port tack.	36 As (31).

8 Instrumentation and electronics

Electronic instrumentation and equipment are an essential part of yacht racing. Knowing how to set up and use your electronic equipment properly will make your boat much faster. This is a fact! Don't be fooled by technophobes who claim electronic equipment is unnecessary to sail a yacht fast. A correctly set up electronic instrumentation system will be far more accurate than your senses.

A minimum system for an offshore boat should include:

- Boatspeed
- Depth
- Apparent wind speed
- Apparent wind angle
- True wind speed
- True wind angle
- True wind direction
- Heading
- VMG (velocity made good)

More sophisticated functions might include :

- Tidal rate and set
- Sea and air temperature
- Barometric pressure
- COG (course over the ground)
- SOG (speed over the ground)
- Leeway
- WCV/VMC (waypoint closure velocity / velocity made down the course)
- Next leg - wind, apparent wind angle and speed
- Polar target speed
- Optimum wind angle
- Rudder angle
- Loadcell readings

Whatever system you have it is vital that you spend time calibrating the instruments as well as getting to know how

to use them. If your boatspeed, apparent wind angle or
electronic compass are not calibrated everything else will
be inaccurate and therefore meaningless.

*This instrumentation is
clearly visible to the whole
crew – excellent!*

Instrument systems can and should be interfaced with the
electronic navigation system giving additional layers of
information. GPS is the most commonly used navigation tool
these days though Loran, Satnav and Decca are still around.

Carry a backup system for navigating the yacht
- these systems are not infallible. You should also
run a further manual check of your position on the
chart - one never knows!

More and more yachts are benefiting from the use of small
computers to integrate onboard systems further. This will
be the way forward in coming years. Custom yacht systems,
which are more robust than the standard PC or laptop, offer
the skipper a huge potential for processing information and
aiding the decision making process.

Inmarsat C, weatherfax, weather routing, satellite imagery,
as well as the more conventional spreadsheets and word
processing facilities can all help the skipper make choices

and manage the yacht better. I imagine that very soon we will have just a screen, mouse and keyboard at the chart table with all yacht instruments controlled and displayed on waterproof touch screen repeaters around the boat.

On *Team Group 4* we equipped the boat with the following :

1. SSB for long range communication, as well as receiving weatherfaxes or satellite images.

2. Weatherfax for dedicated weatherfax, Navtex and satellite reception.

3. Electronic barometer. One of your most important pieces of onboard weather monitoring equipment; should be capable of recording data for at least 24 hours (this one does a week).

4. GPS. A good quality multi-channel GPS is our primary navigating tool.

5. Computer for:
    Inmarsat C reception
    Electronic charting
    Weather routing software
    Weatherfax reception
Other uses limited only by software availability - spreadsheets and word processing.

6. VHF for line-of-sight communications, as well as starting signals and coastal radio weather forecasts.

7. Inmarsat C. Text only communications, weather data reception (Grib files).

8. Inmarsat M/Mini M. Voice communication, also internet access (if allowed) for weather data.

9. Autopilot Control
Out of picture: Radar for monitoring other vessels, including tracking competing yachts for gains and losses. Should be capable of being interfaced with your GPS to allow overlay of waypoints etc.

10. Instrument System - the main full function displays for the B&G instrument system.

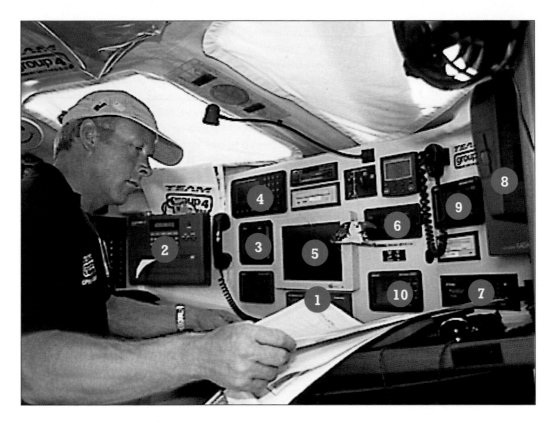

SERVICES AVAILABLE FOR THE OFFSHORE SAILOR

The Navigation Station on *Team Group 4* *(see opposite for description).*

RADIO SERVICES

A large number of services are available and are listed in The Admiralty List of Radio Signals (ALRS) which has six volumes covering all maritime services. Around the UK, coastal radio stations put out regular forecasts on both VHF and SSB radio.

WEATHERFAX

Weatherfax services are listed in ALRS Volume 3 parts 1 and 2. Weatherfax stations around the world are becoming less common. These days large shipping companies are accessing the Internet to get weather information and the need to maintain radio transmission stations has declined. However this is still an excellent service and if you are in a receiving area (Europe is one of the best) this is well worth having.

Weatherfax stations often put out a huge range of `products' which, as well as an analysis of the current weather situation, can include prognosis forecasts for several days ahead. Be selective about what you use, not all 'products' are of the same quality - for instance a 120 hr forecast will not be as reliable as a 24 hr one. Other 'products' include satellite imagery, wind and wave analysis and prognosis, sea temperature and upper air information.

NAVTEX

This is a free system for broadcasting, in printed form, Maritime Safety Information (MSI) eg gale warnings, navigational warnings and weather forecasts.
The broadcasts, on 518 KHz, are made by many of the world's coastal radio stations. You can receive it via SSB on a computer or fit a dedicated receiver/printer.

INMARSAT C

Inmarsat C is a text/data system. It allows the transmission and reception of data from the shore via the Inmarsat satellite system. This system has worldwide coverage and has proved to be extremely reliable. The onboard equipment comprises an ariel and a receiver which has a built-in GPS.

As well as an excellent communication system, Inmarsat C offers an additional safety system with a facility to send an emergency signal at the touch of a button.

GRIB FILES

These are received via Inmarsat C on a subscription basis. The information is specific to an ocean area around your current position. Essentially latitude, longitude, course and speed are transmitted to a land station who will send a 'fan' of information spreading out from your current position. Information available includes :

- Wind fields
- Pressure fields
- Air temperature
- Sea temperature
- Sea state

You can have as much information as you like but you pay for what you receive. I would normally choose a 20 x 20 degree block around my position with six or twelve hour intervals for up to four days ahead. This gives a good idea of what the weather around you is doing.

The biggest benefit of this type of information is the ability, with the right software, to process this information and overlay it on routing and charting programmes. This gives you a visual representation of the wind or pressure fields around your boat and can even offer you guidance on which route will be the best for your yacht's polars. But beware, to make all this happen requires a lot of work. However, I am sure this type of system will be more frequently used and will become simpler to handle as technology develops.

INTERPRETING INCOMING DATA

It's one thing to get your hands on all this data, but another to interpret and put the information to good use. The quality of weather products varies, because of the way the weather maps are produced.

At the local Met Office, the raw data from satellite or observation stations is processed by one or more computer models, which are based on huge amounts of accumulated data from many years of observation. The models turn the raw data into weather charts that are modified further by the forecaster, who knows from experience when and how the model is likely to be incorrect. The finished product is what we see on weather charts and is the product of years of experience and expertise.

For this reason I place little value in looking at satellite imagery and trying to make my own forecast. Some skippers may be able to do this but most will not. I prefer to find high quality products and, together with my local observation of cloud, wind, barometer and temperature, establish where in the system we are and where I expect the system to move to.

In other parts of the world try to find out which model is being used, to assess reliability. Also, look carefully to see at what level the data has been recorded. Some blended charts give upper air data that is of little value, unless you are a meteorologist.

So now you have your data and some idea of how it has been interpreted. What you are really looking for is changes in wind speed and direction. In particular, fronts will have a profound effect (note that the isobars are bent at a front). As a front passes you will move on to a new point of sail and probably need a sail change. You can predict the arrival time by tracking its approach over hours or days.

Watch local conditions and make a note in the log of principal changes every hour, or more often if necessary. This will give a good clue to the speed of approach of the weather systems or fronts.

If, like me, you have trouble remembering all the variables of forecasting refer again to David Houghton's *Wind Strategy* - a very useful book.

A modern CHS yacht.

9 Safety

ATTITUDE

Safety is a topic that is thoroughly covered in publications issued by the RYA. It is not, therefore, my intention to regurgitate lists of things that the skipper should remember and do. It is perhaps more relevant to cover the attitude one must maintain regardless of competitive criteria. As skipper, you are not only responsible for your crew and your yacht but also for other seafarers. It is vital that your actions adhere to the international collision regulations and never put either yourself or others at risk.

It is essential that you don't allow safety to become of secondary importance when racing. So often the competitive streak of the racing sailor reduces the skipper's awareness of even the most basic safety procedures. It is just a matter of time before this leads to problems, the consequences of which could be very serious, even fatal.

Preparing your yacht for any race should always include a thorough check of not only the equipment carried but also the procedures and actions you may adopt in any given situation. Your crew should all be made aware of the equipment and procedures. It is not much use trying to go through what you intend to do to pick up a man overboard (MOB) on a dark and stormy night when the unthinkable has already happened!

It is, however, not always hard and fast rules that work. Individual self-discipline has an important role to play. As in any team sport, everyone should be watching out for themselves and the team, as well as the objective. For example, I may allow the crew to determine when they individually need to wear a lifejacket and safety harness. However, I may demand that they be worn in certain conditions eg higher wind speeds, during the night or in low visibility. Whatever, it is vital that you as skipper 'do as you say'. If you are insisting the crew wear safety equipment make sure you are wearing it as well.

The speed at which the danbouy, horseshoe etc are deployed increases the chances of locating your MOB.

When running large crews I have been known to appoint an on-deck safety officer on each watch. It's a practice from my firefighting days but seems to work. Pick a watch member who is sharp eyed and understands all the procedures.

The main risks that require a degree of preplanning and training are:

- Man overboard (MOB)
- Fire
- Sinking
- Bad weather

MAN OVERBOARD (MOB)

Your Man Overboard Procedure must be practised, practised, practised - not just at the start of the season but throughout the year. It can be fun and challenging for you and your crew to have practical exercises from time to time. Try to make all practical training as realistic as possible and once the basics have been tried in a formal training session try some impromptu exercises throughout the season. Allow

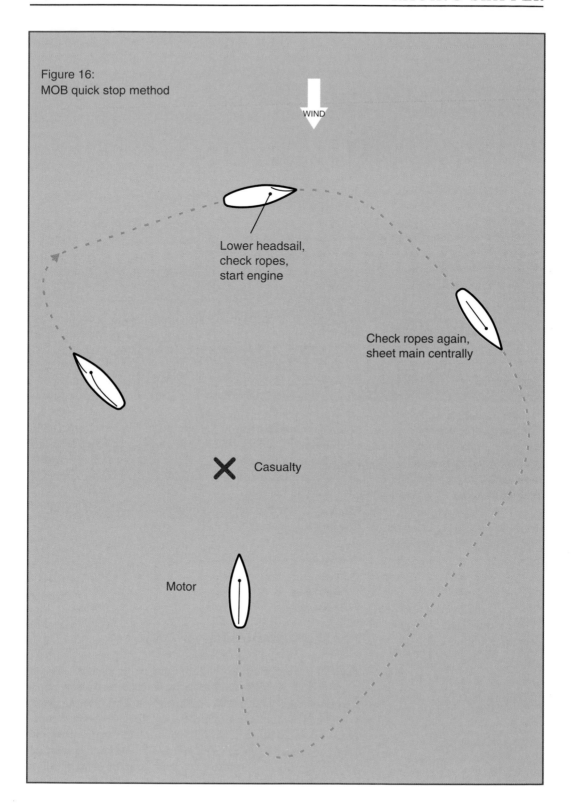

Figure 16:
MOB quick stop method

WIND

Lower headsail,
check ropes,
start engine

Check ropes again,
sheet main centrally

Casualty

Motor

the crew to get on with it without any input from yourself -
after all, you might be the man overboard!

Quick Stop Method of
Man Overboard Recovery

- Prevention is better than cure. Don't let it happen!
- If it does, tack and don't touch anything - effectively
  heaving to.
- Simultaneously throw the safety gear eg a danbuoy
  (perhaps with its own activated personal EPIRB),
  horseshoe, lights and die marker.
- Nominate someone to press the MOB button on the
  GPS, and write down the latitude and longitude in
  the boat's log.
- Designate someone to keep a constant visual on the MOB
  by pointing with arm outstretched. This allows everyone
  in the crew to have a reference as to where the casualty
  is throughout the rescue. It's frightening how quickly
  a person can disappear in big seas.
- Drop the headsail which will be aback and should
  therefore fall directly on deck.
- Check for lines overboard and start the engine.
- To complete the circle to get back to the casualty
  consider tacking rather than gybing if it's too frantic.

Your objective during any MOB is to get back to the
casualty as fast as possible, but under control. This is
definitely a case where more haste is less speed. Either
centre the main and motor upwind towards the MOB, or
approach the MOB at less than one knot on a close reach.
Reduce speed by feathering / easing sheet; gain speed
by sheeting on / bearing away. Recover the casualty on
the leeward side and once alongside get a line to the
MOB if conscious. During the British Steel and BT Global
Challenge round the world races, I appointed one person
on each watch as a designated swimmer who would, if
required, go into the water with line attached to effect a
rescue at the final recovery of the casualty. CPR (Cardio
Pulmonary Respiration) goes hand-in-hand with recovery.
There's no point in recovering someone only to let them
die. In some instances it may be necessary for the swimmer
to put air into the casualty while still in the water.

You will need to have made provision for recovering an MOB.

Options include :

- A halyard, led to the most accessible point.
- A scramble net.
- A Tri-buckle (essentially a canvas triangle, fixed along one edge to the toerail and to a halyard at the opposite corner).

I also recommend pinning up the full MOB procedure on the door of the heads. People need something to read and at least this might save a life!

MOB under spinnaker

Having the kite up is an additional complexity. I would recommend carrying out your conventional drop. Your crew will be used to this and the chances of a massive tangle will be reduced. Make sure while racing that you have everything prepared for an immediate drop. With the spinnaker down proceed as above.

Fire

As a former firefighter I am more aware than most of the hazards of fire. On a yacht you have the major additional

Using the tri-buckle method of MOB recovery has the added benefit of bringing a hypothermic casualty aboard in the horizontal position (a vertical lift could prove fatal).

problem that your route to escape in the event of a serious fire is onto another vessel or into the liferaft. Modern composite yachts can be engulfed in fire and smoke in a matter of seconds and this particular hazard is perhaps one of the most frightening.

Fire is something that can and should be prevented through good housekeeping and regular maintenance. A fire seldom occurs where maintenance has been good and housekeeping is of high quality. It's well worthwhile considering where and how a fire might start on your yacht. Then develop your training and maintenance programme with that in mind.

High fire risk areas on any yacht are:

- Stove and gas installation
- Engine room
- Any electrical installation eg navigation station

Plan your escape route from the boat. Look for dead-end situations and plan the location of your fire protection equipment accordingly. Make sure there is sufficient firefighting equipment. The racing rules will tell you the minimum, but you may decide that you need more - this is not an area to save weight. Lastly, check that everything is in date - fire extinguishers do not have an indefinite life.

SINKING

Even a small hole will sink most yachts very quickly. I have been up to my knees in water on *Group 4* when a half inch sump tank breather pipe blew off during heavy weather. The particular fitting was located behind a trim panel and it took me ages to find and stop the inrush of water. What surprised me most was how quickly a large volume of water found its way into the boat from such a small half inch inlet.

Most common causes?

Fortunately sinking is a fairly rare occurrence but is usually caused by one of the following :

- Grounding - cutting corners while racing.
- Collision - either with other boats, marks of the course or submerged objects.
- Fire - an engine compartment fire may burn through pipework connected to below-waterline skin fittings.
- Structural failure - design faults or collision damage.
- Mechanical failure - such as a hose fitting breaking off.

A few preventative measures for the more common problems :

- Double-clip all skin fitting hoses.
- Exercise all valved through-hull fittings by opening and closing at least monthly to ensure they don't seize.
- Ensure you have the right softwood bungs available in case a through-fitting fails.
- Check that your yacht has an adequate bilge pump system.

For a serious holing you will need to improvise with what you have on board. Again with a little preplanning the standard inventory can be the key to keeping the yacht afloat. For instance, a sail bag held in place with a washboard and a jockey pole to brace across the boat could stem a major hole. If you need additional bilge pump capacity you could consider disconnecting the engine water cooling inlet and using the main engine water pump to help the bilge pump system keep the yacht afloat. In a situation like this 'necessity is the mother of invention'. I've even heard of a yacht sailing across an ocean with a leg of ham jammed into a hole in the hull!

BAD WEATHER

This is a subject on its own, but there are several good books that give instructional accounts of crew actions in extreme weather. Your actions in heavy weather will depend on your crew's experience, the type of yacht you are sailing and your level of preparedness. It's important for you to differentiate between heavy weather - which is a normal part of sailing offshore - and survival conditions which are not. What I mean is that there comes a point at which you must cease to race and focus your attention entirely on the safety of your crew and the yacht. It's difficult to give an indication when this might be - every boat and crew will have a different threshold. It's most important that you, as skipper, realise when the time has come to change your tactics from one to the other.

In general, whether the boat is light or heavy displacement, I prefer to continue sailing in survival conditions. The main reason for this is to maintain the ability to manoeuvre. It's a method I have used to good effect on very light multihulls, which absolutely need the ability to steer through the seas and need sufficient power to climb the next wave. If a multihull starts going backwards then it's got really serious problems. The general philosophy works well even with modern light monohulls which can display many multihull traits.

If you are caught out in tough conditions close everything up, take off sail early and generally ensure your yacht is prepared for an extended blow whatever the forecast. Ensure that the crew's needs continue to be met. Hot food and drinks will smooth your way to surviving bad weather with both morale and yacht intact.

10 Summary

Running a racing yacht involves a tremendous amount of organisation and planning and can be a very complex affair. The bigger the boat and crew, the bigger the issue. Perhaps the best way to deal with it is to adopt a business-like approach to managing the people and the boat. Finding a method of managing that works and getting it right is tremendously satisfying.

The following is a synopsis of the key elements of this book :

• Selecting the right people

Like any project or business venture, the quality of the people around you will affect the outcome. Choose your crew carefully to get the right balance and make sure they are compatible with one another.

• Leading the campaign

As skipper you will be expected to lead from the front but it is important to involve your crew in the management process too. Agree goals and values. Give everyone an individual area of responsibility and encourage support of one another. Also ensure good communications both on and off the water.

• Training and motivating the crew

Treat every sailing session as an opportunity to gain knowledge and experience. After sailing get your crew together and debrief the session in its entirety. Let everyone have their say, have the session minuted and ensure everyone gets a copy of these notes before the next sail. Then, with the business over, head for the bar !

Photo: © Yachting World

"As sailors, we can always count on volunteer lifeboat crews. Can they count on you? Please join *Offshore* today."

Sir Robin Knox-Johnston CBE, RD*

However experienced you are at sea, you never know when you'll need the help of a lifeboat crew. But to keep saving lives, the Royal National Lifeboat Institution's volunteer crews need *your* help.

That is why you should join **Offshore**. For just £3.50 per month, you can help save thousands of lives, receive practical information to help keep *you* safe at sea *and* save money on equipment for your boat. *Please join us today.*

Please join *Offshore* – today

Please photocopy and return this form, with your payment if appropriate, to: RNLI, FREEPOST, West Quay Road, Poole, Dorset BH15 1XF.

Mr/Mrs/Miss/Ms ☐ Initial ☐ Surname ☐

Address ☐

Postcode ☐

I would like to join:

☐ As an *Offshore* member at £ ☐ per month/quarter/year * (min £3.50 per month/£10 per quarter/£40 per year)

☐ As Joint *Offshore* members at £ ☐ per month/quarter/year *

(Husband & Wife, min £6 per month/£17.50 per quarter/£70 per year) * please delete as applicable

Please debit the above sum as indicated from my Visa/MasterCard * now and at the prevailing rate until cancelled by me in writing.

Card No. ☐☐☐☐☐☐☐☐☐☐☐☐☐☐☐☐ Expiry date ☐ / ☐

Signature ☐ (Please give address of cardholder on a separate piece of paper if different from above.)

Alternatively, I wish to pay my **Offshore** membership by cheque/PO

I enclose a cheque/Postal Order for £ ☐ payable to Royal National Lifeboat Institution.

Or, I wish to pay my subscription by Direct Debit ☐

Please tick the box – a Direct Debit form will be sent to you.   FERN2

Lifeboats
Offshore

Because life's not all plain sailing

Registered Charity No. 209603

• Managing your budget

Yacht racing is an expensive sport but by pre-planning your campaign carefully and making good choices you can make significant savings. Above all you must make the correct choice of class and race area to suit the budget available. There is nothing worse than finding yourself with the costs of your campaign spiralling out of control.

• Getting on with the racing

At some point you have to make a real start, put the theory into practice and get out on the race course. Don't be disheartened when things go wrong - it's all part of the learning curve. Remember: skippering a racing yacht should be **FUN** and hopefully, with a little pre-planning and preparation, **SUCCESSFUL** too!

GET OUT ON THE RACE COURSE AND ENJOY IT !